The Young Author Festival Handbook

What Every Planner Needs to Know

Marguerite Cogorno Radencich
Kathleen Oropallo

bee line
BOOKS

Heinemann
Portsmouth, NH

To all of the teachers from whom I have learned.
—M.C.R.

To the 1990–1991 Cayuga Street School fourth-grade
teaching team, and to Mom and Dad.
—K.O.

Heinemann
A division of Reed Elsevier Inc.
361 Hanover Street
Portsmouth, NH 03801–3912
http://www.heinemann.com

Offices and agents throughout the world

Library of Congress Cataloging-in-Publication Data
Radencich, Marguerite C., 1952–1998
     The young author festival handbook : what every planner needs to
  know / Marguerite Cogorno Radencich, Kathleen Oropallo.
       p.   cm.
  Includes bibliographical references.
  ISBN 0-325-00020-4
    1. Creative writing–United States.   2. Festivals–United States–
Planning.   3. English language–Composition and exercises–Study
and teaching (Elementary)–United States.   4. Education, Elementary–
Activity programs–United States.   I. Oropallo, Kathleen.
II. Title.
LB1576.R258   1999   98-46243
                                                   CIP

Editor: Leigh Peake
Production: Elizabeth Valway
Interior design: Greta D. Sibley & Associates
Text illustrations: Kathleen Oropallo (Figures 1–2, 1–4, 1–5, 1–6, 2–1, and 3–1)
Cover design: Darci Mehall/Aureo Design
Manufacturing: Louise Richardson

Contents

Preface

> I must write. I must write at all costs, for writing is more
> than living. It is being conscious of living.
>
> —Anne Morrow Lindberg

Yes! Students are *real* authors! What better way to help children perceive themselves that way than by giving them an audience at a young authors' festival? What better way to encourage them to perfect the content and format of their writing and to develop poise in oral presentation? First established in the late 1970s, writers' festivals, conferences, day camps, and teas have since become quite fashionable, and for good reason. The core of these events is students reading their writing to others. But the events are often much more. There is much to consider in successfully putting together a young authors' festival, as there is with any event.

    We conceived the idea for *The Young Author Festival Handbook* after hosting twelve hundred students at our day long Suncoast Young Authors' Celebration. Margie was slumped in an armchair and Kathy in a recliner. Half jokingly, Kathy suggested an article on our process, and Margie said, "Why not a book?" We had talked previously about preparing a handbook for our local colleagues who might take on the festival when we gave it up. But we realized that the need was not just a local one. Between us we had planned many events from gatherings in our own elementary classrooms to district-level young authors' festivals and state-level conferences for adults, and had always found a handbook made the task much smoother. We have learned from experience that good long-term organization must undergird the collaboration and the passion.

We write this book with honesty about our successes and foibles alike. We begin with a chapter on the year-long writing activities which precede the successful writing found at the best young authors' festivals. We then discuss the most common form of young authors' festival, one held during the school year at one school site. Interspersed are hints from teachers, comments from festival participants, and adaptations of these procedures to individual classroom festivals. Later in the book, we provide a chapter on larger-scale festivals at a district level or for all of the elementary and middle schools that feed into one particular high school. Throughout all chapters are references to which forms are in the Appendix.

As you consider holding a young authors' festival, you will be faced with many decisions. One relates to timing. You should give young authors enough time to gather some writings before the festival, whether your event is a young writers' summer camp or one or several festivals held during the school year. You will want to consider whether festival participation should be selective, or whether all students should be involved. You should invite an outside author if possible, but young authors' festivals can also be quite successful with just home-bred talent. You should consider gathering student work into a class or school anthology. The different possibilities may leave your head swimming with excitement! Good luck and happy writing!

We wish to thank first the initiators of the Suncoast Young Authors' Conference at the University of South Florida and at institutions everywhere. These pioneers led the way. We thank also writers of conference handbooks in state councils of the International Reading Association. We borrowed many ideas from one such handbook, that of the Florida Reading Association. Finally, we thank all those who have lovingly toiled with us in making our festivals come to pass.

We hope you will gather from this book ideas that will help you with your own young authors' festival. Write on!

Chapter 1

Setting the Stage for a Young Authors' Festival

 **Introduction**

Many of us looking back on our own experiences with writing remember practicing letter formations, writing to prompts like how we spent our summer vacations, and having a paper strewn with red pen marks over mechanical errors. But some of us can think back to a time when we got out construction paper and crayons or markers on a rainy day, and began to construct books of stories or poems. Pulling a favorite book off the shelf, we may have copied the story verbatim and approximated the illustrations, grabbed a stapler or some glue, and presto—our own book! The storyline was one we had probably memorized from our parent's repeated reading, so we excitedly read and reread our "book" to them. Oftentimes, our parents stuffed that creation in a drawer or file for safekeeping, and the moment left an indelible image of delight. Or maybe it was a moment as a teenager, going through the angst of change, finding a hidden moment to write a poem, tormented by an unrequited first love or the feeling that we alone were facing the bitter challenges of "teenage-dom." Sometimes we would slip these pieces of ourselves to a best friend in study hall or share them with a small group of friends.

These were very different experiences, marking our attitudes about what real writing was. Unfortunately, the "real" writing in our minds was the writing done in school, and the latter examples were seen as play, make-believe, or emotional release. What was it about our home writing that made us not see it as authentic? What was it about these experiences that compelled us to seek out some kind of audience? Can you recall any of these moments yourself? Lucy Calkins (1994) writes:

> When we, as teachers, do not have good memories of writing to draw upon, we are apt to accept our students' resistance to writing as a given. When we assume that writing will always be a dreaded activity, we spend all our time pushing, luring, motivating, and bribing. . . . We cannot teach writing well unless we trust that there are real, human reasons to write. . . . If we have even once in our lives experienced the power of writing, our teaching will be changed forever. (11–13)

The power of writing? What does Lucy Calkins mean? We have seen this power in working with students and teachers over the past few years inviting them to write and share in young authors' festivals. Jonathan, a ten-year-old who wouldn't pick up a pencil in September, remembers the death of the dog that was his companion and best friend in a six-page book. Rikki, a prolific ten-year-old writer, in her eight-chapter book, tells of the hide-and-seek adventure with her younger sister and friends. She later writes a sequel entitled, *When April and I Play Hide-n-Seek II.* Benjamin, a first grader, who had begun the year very reluctant to write had, by December 1, written a quite creditable report on the Navajos. Nola, a classroom teacher of twenty-plus years, tells of her first experience at freedom and the lesson she learned about it at the age of eighteen months. This is a small sample of her memoir:

> My first taste of freedom also is my earliest recollection. I was about eighteen months old. My family consisted of my father, mother, and brother, who was five years to the day older than myself. Dad was a Baptist preacher, and Mother was a homemaker. She was my protector, and

> The Navado
> women made
> Yarn.
> The Navado men
> huntled.

now that I look back over the years I'm sure she watched over me like a mother hen did in those days keeping her babies safe from chicken hawks. We lived in a parsonage in which the preacher and his family lived. . . .

The door of the house flew open, and my mother with several ladies in tow came screaming out into the yard. Mother snatched me up. She did not worry about the blood and the mess I was causing on her clothes. She screamed, "Get Howard." Howard was my dad. He was one who always maintained control. They got our Model A Ford, bustled me into it, and drove as fast as they could to Osceola, Arkansas, to Dr. Massey. Here my memory fades. From what my mom and dad told me, I was taken to the doctor, and he sewed up my knee. I still have the scar. I still find myself rushing into situations too fast and getting hurt, but I'm learning to stop and look before I leap. Freedom to do what you want is not always the easiest and safest thing to possess. Freedom without being responsible leaves scars.

When we write about subjects that are meaningful to us and when we have a sense of audience, someone listening to our words, we come to know what Donald Murray says, "Expect the unexpected." It is in the surprises that emerge that we come to know ourselves as writers and the power of writing. As teachers we can provide opportunity for children to experience and know this power firsthand. By writing daily in the classroom and celebrating writing as part of a literate community, we encourage children to explore the world around them and share the storied lives they bring into our classrooms.

To help our students to feel like real writers, we can begin to examine what real writers do and provide opportunities for our young writers to engage in similar processes and interactions. We can provide different kinds of audiences for their writing.

Imagine a room full of children proudly clutching small handmade books that contain crayon illustrations and text. Stories of pets, sports, family travel, and friendship fill the pages. Small groups of children smile, curiously watching and listening to one other. Each child slowly gathers courage, reading from the curled pages and holding up his/her book for all to see. Imagine watching each of them almost puff up with pride before your very eyes, knowing the joy of being an author. The certificates marking their participation are placed on a refrigerator or bulletin board. Years later, these certificates are still kept as a token of shared literacy, as a token of writerly accomplishment. Imagine these children, now taller and in the middle grades, reading their quite sophisticated writing to an appreciative audience.

We share two quotes, one of a student and one of a teacher, regarding the power of young authors' festivals:

> I like authors' tea because you can hear other people's stories and people clap for the effort you put in, and it makes me feel good inside. . . . Listen to my stories. You might get some good ideas and be surprised. It's my dream to be an author.
>
> —Fifth-Grade Young Author

> I think it's very empowering for students to realize that they can be recognized for their writing and their art. We've taken advantage of our connections at the Design and Architecture High School and had Gloria and Jerry Pinkney [talk to students]. The festivals are a good way for

kids to visualize themselves as writers. That's the key. I think they're a lot of fun. Also, they open up career directions in high school. That's how we promote them. One of these days we'll get a student who chooses to write or illustrate children's books as a career. One of these days.

—Debra Miller, Senior High School
Reading Teacher

As students prepare for the authentic audience that is a young authors' festival, they have a purpose for perfecting the form and content of their writing and for developing poise in oral presentation. A young authors' festival may also give young writers the opportunity to meet professionally published authors and gain insight into the authoring process. Harste and Short with Burke (1995) write:

> Students' recognition of themselves as authors is facilitated when they have the chance to meet professionally published authors or when they hear and read about the lives and the authoring processes of professional authors. These professional authors may be writers, poets, or illustrators. Students begin to see professional authors as real people who have to work hard at their authoring and who encounter difficulties, just as students do. Learning about and meeting authors demystifies the authoring process and opens students up to exploring different strategies in their own writing and illustrating. (403)

This kind of celebration moves young writers beyond regular classroom interaction and offers the audience of writers and listeners the privilege of hearing the writer read his/her own written text.

In hosting over twelve hundred students in a young authors' festival, we have come to understand with all the planning, organizing, and preparation, what makes an effort like this a success: The voices of the writers and the audience of listeners leave students empowered as writers and us empowered as advocates of literacy. Neither the size of the festival nor the participation of an outside author means more than that.

Ways to Support a Community of Writers

A writing celebration is the result of ongoing literacy practices beginning with the establishment of a writing community. This sets the stage for a collaborative endeavor that centers on writing models, exposure to the various genres and writing styles in good literature, conversation, and risk-free sharing. The spark for creating such a reading/writing culture can be set in the classroom or at the school or district level. Supporting this culture involves an open invitation to all members of the school communtiy: children, media specialists, classroom and resource teachers, building support personnel, and administrators. We share here classroom-tested activities and strategies to help you create your own community of writers!

Activities to Support Emergent Writers

You can support emergent writers in a myriad of ways as they experiment with print. Children can be invited to write in every learning center in the classroom. Have paper and pencils available for phone messages, for orders in a fast-food restaurant, for grocery lists posted on a refrigerator. Have a sign-in clipboard by the classroom door. At times the chalkboard or a large sheet of butcher block paper can provide a reluctant writer the security of a community effort. Slates and individual chalkboards are also reassuring because of the impermanence of the recording. Classrooms which encourage emergent writers are chock-full of words—student names, labels, word walls—which children may refer to in their writing.

You will be able, with a little encouragement, to move a scribble to something resembling letters, or a meaningless letter string to the beginnings of letter–sound correspondence, or an *I love you* spelled as *ILU* to *I LV U* and eventually to *I LUV U* and then to conventional spelling. You accomplish this movement as you provide multiple daily opportunities for exploring with print, as you bend over the shoulder of individual children, as you model and talk about writing during a news-of-the-day module, and as you remind students of the print around them during a read-around-the-room segment. Children can mix and match forms of writing, depending on individual needs. Consider the following adapted from Clay (1975):

- Draw pictures to which you attach dictated captions.
- Trace over your handwriting.
- Copy captions.
- Copy words around the room.
- Write "remembered" word forms down independently.
- Write invented (generated) word forms, often correctly.
- Get written copy of unknown words from you.
- Get occasional (once a week) group lessons on letter formation.
- Get individual guidance on letter formation daily.

 Authors' Profiles

Children can learn much as they enjoy exploring individual professional authors and/or illustrators. Just as we return to old favorites, we can spur children to do the same.

◉ How Does Profiling an Author Help Me Teach Writing?

Profiling an author gives children insight into the secrets of the writer's craft, from "How do you find your ideas?" to "Did that really happen?" With author or illustrator profiles, students learn that Faith Ringgold wrote of her childhood experience on a tar roof, and that Byrd Baylor lives without electricity, and that

Jerry Pinkney uses his family members as models. Students identify with the author when they know that the author is still alive, likes cats, and lives in the country. Students see how an author's life influences his/her work. Specifically, author profiles help writing in the following ways:

- Professional authors model writing habits for children.
- Author-shared insights can be transformed into minilessons.
- Students are better able to understand that we write for an audience, and that audiences differ.
- The process of writing takes time and is challenging, and even published writers get writer's block.
- Writers are ordinary people (like them)!
- Students learn to READ with a WRITER'S EYE!

Media specialist Libby Miller shares her school's experience with a guest author at her school:

> We invite an author every year to our book fairs. We're lucky that Miami has a large book fair every year and that we can piggyback on the authors who come. One year we invited Jack Gantos, the author of *Rotten Ralph*, and children had to write a sequel to the book. We selected 60 students whose writing had the best beginning, middle, and end. These students were selected to go listen to him. Last year we had Emily Arnold McCully, the author of *Mirette on the High Wire*. The children wrote letters. It's important that they learn how to write letters to an author! Those with the best letters go to hear her speak.

> —Libby Miller, Media Specialist

◎ Where Do I Get Information on Authors/Illustrators?

You can try a search engine like http://www.yahoo.com to find information about an author on the Internet. Your media specialist is another source. Some teachers and media specialists keep ongoing files of information about authors/illustrators. They cut out sheets on authors/illustrators from teacher magazines. They keep notes from talks at festivals. They collect author/illustrator information at conferences and bookstores. Frequenting bookstores also helps them keep up with new titles by favorite authors.

Some media specialists help the school get to know authors/illustrators. Media specialists know that Jan Brett sends out delightful illustrated brochures on each new book to anyone who writes to her (132 Pleasant Street, Norwell, MA 02061). They can help find authors who keep Web pages such as Virginia Hamilton (http://members.aol.com/bodeep.inex.html) and Avi (http://www.avi-writer.com). Media specialists may prepare displays of books written by an author, highlight an author/illustrator over morning announcements, prepare collections for use by classrooms, and obtain free materials from the publisher on the author/illustrator. With the information at hand, media specialists may be the ones to point out that some piece of his dog appears in all, or almost all, of Chris Van Allsburg's books, or that each *Arthur* book of Marc Brown's contains the names of his children somewhere in the illustrations.

Here is a list of sources that can help you become an author expert. See the References section at the end of the book for ordering information.

Teacher Resources

- Scholastic, Troll, and Trumpet Book Club flyers
- Scholastic and Trumpet Book Club audiotapes
- Videotapes by American School Publishers, Houghton Mifflin, Owen, Scholastic, Silver Burdett Ginn, and Trumpet Books

Reference Materials

- Gale Research's *Something about the Author*
- SRA's *Once upon a Time* (primary) and *Long Ago and Far Away* (intermediate)
- Scholastic's *Meet the Authors and Illustrators* (elementary)
- The National Council of Teachers of English's *Speaking for Ourselves: Autobiographical Sketches by Notable Authors of*

Books for Young Adults and *Speaking for Ourselves, Too: More Autobiographical Sketches* . . . (intermediate and above), and *Getting to Know You: Profiles of Children's Authors Featured in Language Arts 1985–1990* (elementary)

- Silvey, Anita. 1995. *Children's Books & Their Creators: A Companion.* Boston: Houghton.

For additional collections, see the International Reading Association's *Research and Professional Resources in Children's Literature.*

Magazines

- *Book Links, The Horn Book, Instructor, Language Arts, The New Advocate, Teaching K–8*

Books That Feature Children as Authors

An often-overlooked inspiration for writing is books which feature children as authors. Have students read and discuss books about children who like to write. Younger children will enjoy the letter exchanges in Ezra Jack Keats' *A Letter to Amy* or Simon James' *Dear Mr. Blueberry.* They can see different types of models in Arthur, who in Marc Brown's *Arthur Meets the President* has won a writing contest; Amelia, who in M. Moss' *Amelia's Notebook* uses journal entries to cope with her family's move and other changes in her life; or Lily, who in Palmyra LoMonaco's *Night Letters* takes her notepad to her backyard where she reads and copies messages left by insects, trees, and rocks. They can read explanations of the processes used by children's authors in books like Janet Stevens' *From Pictures to Words: A Book About Making a Book.* And they can learn of the obstacles that Helen Lester faced from age three to adulthood in *Author: A True Story.*

Intermediate- or middle-school students will also enjoy the picture books. In addition, they have as models Harriet's notes in Louise Fitzhugh's *Harriet the Spy,* Leigh's letters and diary entries in Beverly Cleary's *Dear Mr. Henshaw* and its sequel *Strider,* Sam's journal entries of his questions and of significant events in E. B. White's *The Trumpet of the Swan,* Birdy's diary entries in Karen Cushman's *Catherine, Called Birdy*, or the letters of children around the United States in Jean Stubbs' *Dear Laura: Letters From Children to Laura Ingalls Wilder*. They will also enjoy memoirs of popular children's authors such as Yoshiko Uchida's *The Invisible Thread*, Jean Fritz's *Homesick: My Own Story*, and Amy Ehrlich's *When I Was Your Age* which are stories based on real incidents that happened to children's authors during their childhood.

 **Read-Alouds**

Reading aloud to students can help them hear an author's voice and to appreciate crafted writing as entertainment. In your daily read-alouds, pause periodically to appreciate or highlight a writer's ability. Although we do not encourage interruption that interferes with the story itself, momentary pauses to reread a passage or line and discuss the artfulness of the segment can allow children as well as teachers to delight in the sounds, descriptions, and rhythm of a writer's language. One can't help but pause and savor the opening to Eleanora Tate's *A Blessing in Disguise*:

> Check this out: Here I was again, on the Friday afternoon of Fourth of July weekend. I had nothing to do again but sit on my bike in the middle of dull, dusty Silver Dollar Road. Worse, I was still in itsy-bitsy, countrified, do-nothing Deacons Neck, South Carolina.

Or, once you have paused after, say, the initial appearance of the "life as a wheel" metaphor in Natalie Babbitt's *Tuck Everlasting*, you might simply slow down at recurrences of the metaphor to clue students in to its appearance, and then allow them to bring up this author's device later in their conversations.

Use picture books with young and older students alike by reading the story once for plot and general enjoyment and then returning to it to celebrate author's craft. Thus, you might point out that Mem Fox believes the rhythms in the Bible have led to the rhythm in her writing or that Jane Yolen's similes in *Owl Moon* were born of her own experience with owling.

 **Book Talks**

One of the quickest ways to expose your students to excellent writing is to do short, daily book talks. Book talks can be as simple as reading a single paragraph or page from a book and giving a brief summary of the book. In essence, we snuck book talks in the last section when we gave you reasons to look closely at a few choice titles.

The more you know about children's literature, the more you can use book talks to help with student writing. With an intermediate student having trouble creating sentence variety, you can turn to Katherine Paterson as a model, or you can send a younger child needing a pattern to follow to Charles Remy's *Fortunately*. You can elicit a sense of mystery while asking children to uncover the hidden story in a Chris Van Allsburg book. For example, in *The Mysteries of Harris Burdick*, the author discovers a storyteller's artwork and singular phrases that depict something about the untold story left in the pictures. You don't, however, need to be this specific. Just doing book talks to expose students to good literature will give them excellent models for their writing as a whole.

Teachers aren't the only ones who can give book talks! Invite school personnel into your classroom each week to share a favorite book. Everyone from the secretary to the custodian probably has at least one favorite book that they could share with your class. Make book talks fun. We know of one resource teacher who did book talks from atop a tree. And don't forget the most believable book talk givers—students themselves. Students can share favorites perhaps in a round-robin session or over a brown bag lunch. Enjoy—and read for yourself—the new discoveries that will emerge!

Writers' Workshops

One way young writers achieve a sense of authorship is by having real reasons to write, writing on a daily basis, and having an audience to share and respond to writing. The writers' workshop is a recursive approach to writing in which students move through the stages of the writing process and are engaged in writerly activities. The classroom becomes much like an artist's studio where writers come to work their craft at their own pace and in their own style. One key to a successful writers' workshop is to engage young authors to write on a daily basis. Calkins (1994) notes: "When we teach writing, we first establish simple, predictable writing workshops and then move about the classroom extending what our students do." She goes on to say, "Our teaching is characterized not by the words we say but by the ongoing structures and rituals that shape the writing workshop" (32).

In a typical writers' workshop, the teacher starts with a quick roll call in which each student shares where he/she is at in the writing process. This is called a status-of-the-class conference (Atwell 1987). By beginning a writers' workshop with status-of-the-class, teachers ask young writers to make a commitment to their day's writing. The workshop then proceeds with the following components (Calkins 1994), in no particular order.

- **teacher minilessons** of approximately ten minutes duration for instruction and modeling on topics the teacher has noted from student writing as needing instruction or topics that students are expected to learn at their grade level

- **ample time for writing and conferencing**, including both peers and teacher conferences at any stage of the writing process

- **authors' chair**, a special chair used by student authors when they have questions to ask of the community of writers that their class has become or to use when they share their writing with their classmates and seek their reactions

◉ How Do I Manage a Writers' Workshop with My Students?

There are three elements that are key to a successful writers' workshop: time, choice, and predictability. Here are some tips to managing a writers' workshop:

- Begin and end the workshop as a whole class to establish and reinforce the concept of a writing community.

- Find a predictable time for daily writing. When children have predictable times to write, they anticipate writing, think about possible topics, and "write when they are not writing" (Calkins 1987, 28).

- Gradually scaffold opportunities for students to make choices. Students can select writing topics, which pieces to develop and which to abandon, which suggestions of others to incorporate into their writing, where changes might be placed in a piece, ways of publishing a piece, and which piece(s) to share during a young authors' festival.

- Provide a writing center in your classroom. All writers need tools to mold their craft. Include: various types of writing paper, pens, and markers as well as publishing materials such as construction paper, glue, tape, yarn, wallpaper, and reference books.

- Create a print-rich environment that includes word walls organized for easy access to needed words, writing topic lists, examples of published and unpublished writing, labels, and have-a-go cards.

- Model writing and share examples of good writing on a daily basis. This can be done through minilessons, book talks, or simply discussing good literature as students read or are read to.

- Provide regular time for authors' chair. Some teachers use the TAG procedure to help students respond in authors' chair (Tell something you heard, Ask a question, Give a suggestion). Children who are used to participating in authors' chair will find sharing during a young authors' festival to be less intimidating than would otherwise be the case.

Organizational Tools

Without organization, there can be no writing program. Use writing folders and organizational sheets to help you and your students keep track of class writing.

Writing Folders

Nancie Atwell (1987), a longtime teacher of writing, suggests a management system for writing that enables teacher and student to follow the writing process over time. This system of management is often operated by the students themselves and helps organize teacher tracking and record-keeping throughout the year.

The Daily Folder

The daily folder holds writing the students work on every day. All current stages of process writing are included. Folders should be stored in a place which allows students easy access.

The Permanent Folder

The permanent folder stores all finished pieces of writing, old drafts, webs, etc. "Nothing is thrown away" is the rule in writers' workshop.

 Organizational Sheets

Organizational sheets are invaluable in keeping track of writers' workshop. Each teacher's sheets will be different. Here are some suggestions:

Writing Folders Conference Sheet

To monitor daily writing, most teachers who use writers' workshop examine six folders a day, focusing on one main area of need for each student. The teacher then meets with the six students first at the start of writers' workshop. Attention to only one area at a time during the student-teacher conference enables the student to focus.

Status-of-the-Class Sheet

The status-of-the-class sheet is used to monitor the stage of process writing at which each student is working. This sheet functions as a place to record student commitment to the writers' workshop time.

Writers' Conference Sign-Up Sheet

To monitor peer conferencing, students sign up for either an ear conference (Does it sound right, or does it need revision?) or an eye conference (Does it look right, or does it need editing?) with a partner. These conferences generally last no longer than fifteen minutes, depending on the length of the piece.

Writing Partnerships

A wonderful way to explore audience is through same-age or cross-age writing partnerships. When students have a real audience, they become more engaged in the authorship process. When partners are of the same age, partnerships can provide yearlong supportive communities. When older students model writing for younger children, all begin to see themselves as writers. Older students become supporters of individuals moving through process writing, giving advice and feedback along the way. Older students for whom writing is difficult find themselves being the helper for a change. Younger students might share what they have learned from an author study, teaching older students about a new author in the process. Or they might share their synonym wall, spurring their older partners to create one of their own. Partners might design together the layout of a picture book, perhaps with one being the author and the other the illustrator. Partners listen carefully to each other's words, give each other insights, and cheer each other on.

◎ How Can I Organize Writing Partnerships?

Students can be paired with buddies in a number of different ways.

Grouping	Purpose
Multiage Pairing	• To expose younger children to process writing
	• To provide opportunities for less proficient writers to build confidence in writing in a noncompetitive environment
Cross-Class Pairing	• To build communities of writers and provide a regular authentic audience for their writing
	• To build confidence of reluctant writers
Classroom Buddies	• To provide writers with a focused sense of support for conferring, audience response, prewriting, drafting, and revising
Cross-Generational	• To share common and unique experiences that can be transformed into personal narratives and memoirs

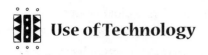

Use of Technology

Today's technologies include marrying the stand-alone computer with videodisc players, CD-ROM drives, scanners, video and audio digitizers, modems, and television—hence the term *multimedia*. Technology changes so quickly that no list of recommended materials can remain current for long. For reviews, consult reading/language arts publications as well as technological publications such as *Electronic Learning* (Scholastic) and *Technology and Learning* (2451 East River Road, Dayton, OH 45439). Here are examples of ways students can use technology as both a tool and a reference for enhancing writing.

◎ Computer Software

Many software programs make desktop publishing a relatively easy endeavor. Both graphics and text can be interwoven to create published pieces of writing with a professional look. Other programs integrate writing with other features. For example, Scholastic's *Wiggleworks* integrates storybooks, beginning reading and writing skills, and portfolios. Intermediate- to middle-school programs like *The Oregon Trail* and *The Amazon Trail* by MECC and *The Lost Tribe* (Lawrence Publications), though primarily social studies oriented, can be used to enhance writing and reading skills in cooperative group decision-making settings. Particularly useful are CD-ROM encyclopedias such as *Grolier's Multimedia Encyclopedia* (Grolier—IBM/Macintosh/Apple), which brings reference work to life for elementary and secondary students by using digitized pictures, animation, and video clips. An elementary reference tool called *First Connection: The Golden Book Encyclopedia* (Hartley—Macintosh) contains a built-in notebook for note taking and reads all or selected text aloud to the student.

◎ E-mail

Students who have access to computer networks within or beyond the school can dialogue with each other. One multiage classroom placed various forms of poetry on the district network and received hundreds of responses from teachers, administrators, and students who read their work. Students can write KidPub@KidPub.org, a part of the Alphabet Superhighway to communicate with other writers.

◉ Internet

Students using networked computers can be linked to the Internet and the World Wide Web. The Internet posts thousands of entry sites that students can explore. As of the date of this writing, one possibilitiy is the Alphabet Superhighway at http://www.kidpuborg.kidpub/ that provides multiple opportunities for young writers. Students can read stories of other children and can participate in online publishing themselves. This Web site includes writing contests, pen pals, webzines with articles, poems, book reviews, and ideas. It publishes both individual and class writing. Other Internet examples are sites in which students can tour famous museums, hear authors read their work, see Shakespearian plays performed, and access facts on topics such as rain forest deforestation. The Internet provides access to libraries all over the world. Useful for all age groups is a subscription to *WorldClassroom* (Global Learning Corporation), a global online computer education network that enables students to use real-life data in core curriculum projects to make decisions about themselves and their environment. To order, write to Global Learning Corporation, P.O. Box 201361, Arlington, TX 76006.

Keep ethical considerations in mind when using technology. David Thornburg has noted that students can create "shovelware" of their own, pounding out a three-hundred-page tome on virtually any subject by downloading material from the Internet, dressing it up with a few well-chosen images, and pasting on a custom title page. Following is a tip to keep in mind (Radencich & Schumm 1997):

> It's *legal* to cut-and-paste portions of a copyrighted program, such as a video image, into an original presentation; it's *illegal* to present downloaded information verbatim as one's own writing.

◼ Getting Ready to Celebrate: Bookmaking Tips

Setting the stage for celebrating writing by publishing student-made books can be one of the most enjoyable aspects of the sharing of writing. Children involved in the book publishing process can gain further insight into authorship and understand how a piece of writing is transformed and delivered to an audience.

Book publishing really goes beyond the creation of a book. It involves teaching young authors about book components, the careful blending of the work of author and illustrator, and the various other people who work together to produce a book. Understanding the entire process helps students understand why the writers' market is so competitive and why books can sometimes be expensive. This information will be especially helpful to students considering careers in the field. A great book that illustrates the bookmaking process is Aliki's *How a Book Is Made*. This picture book takes young authors all the way through the bookmaking process from start to finish and introduces them to the various people responsible for helping a piece of writing become a book. We have found this book useful in introducing students to a classroom publishing center.

◎ Modeling Book Contents and Layout

Of course a good book begins with an effective piece of writing, but when young authors begin to publish, they may not know of other parts of books such as title pages, dedication pages, tables of contents, glossaries, introductions, author pages, or even prologues and epilogues. Challenge students to find these pages in the books that they read. As they do so, ask them, "What elements are the same and different? What are the qualities and characteristics of these pages? What information do they provide?"

We always find it helpful to make this a minilesson and to challenge students to some self-discovery. Following this, we then choose some examples, and turn them into overhead transparencies, and share them with the class. We explain why different genres may hold different pages. For example, narratives might have prologues as in Gary Paulsen's *The Winter Room* or epilogues as in Natalie Babbitt's *Tuck Everlasting*, whereas many nonfiction books will require glossaries. We also discuss that a title page is the one page included in all books.

Ways to Publish Books

No-Glue Paper Bag Books

Materials: brown or white paper sandwich bags or large grocery bags

Step 1: Fold paper bag in half

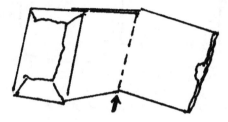

Step 2: Cut slit to right and left of bag fold.

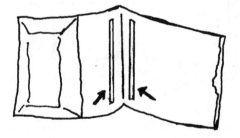

Step 3: Cut white paper to fit. Fold in half.

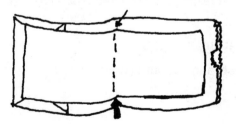

Step 4: Cut two square notches at top and bottom of the paper fold. The paper is now ready for students' writing.

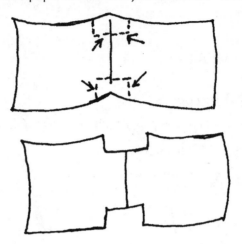

Step 5: Insert students' writing into slits of bag.

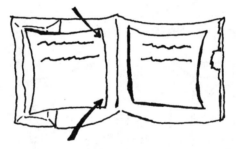

Tri-Fold Books

Materials: Book patterns, stapler or glue (only for pocketbooks), white construction paper

Step 1: Trace pattern onto paper.

Step 2: Fold paper and cut out pattern.

Step 3: Add text.

Ziploc Books

Materials: Ziploc Baggies (size of choice), tape or clips

Step 1: Decide how many pages you will need.

Step 2: Count out Baggies and tape or clip together on side other than sealed side. Tape every joint.

Step 3: Insert students' writing.

Hardcover Books

Materials: wallpaper or contact paper, large paintbrushes, glue-water mixture, cardboard or cereal boxes, yarn, tape, white drawing paper

Step 1: Cut cardboard to size of front cover. Cut wallpaper/contact paper to allow approximately 1½ inch margins beyond size of cardboard.

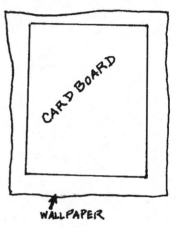

Step 2: Place wallpaper/contact paper underneath cardboard and fold back two horizontal edges. Paste contact paper or glue wallpaper with glue-water mixture using large paintbrushes.

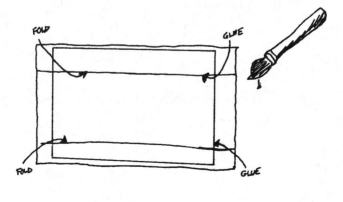

Step 3: Cut off corners of paper on short sides of rectangle. Cut from corner to center (resembling the roof of a house).

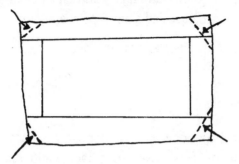

Step 4: Fold cut edges over and glue down.

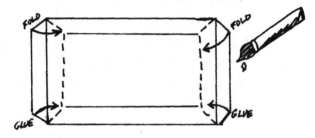

Step 5: Cut piece of white paper to fit over the cardboard with ½ inch margin on all sides. Glue.

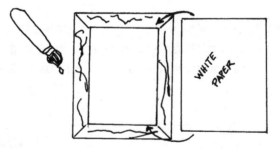

Step 6: Three-hole punch and repeat steps 1–6 for back cover.

Step 7: Add three-hole-punched writing pages. Tie with yarn.

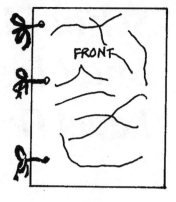

Chapter 2

School-Level and Classroom-Level Festivals

> For me, it is essential that children are deeply involved in writing, that they share their texts with others, and that they perceive themselves as authors. I believe these three things are interconnected. A sense of authorship comes from the struggle to put something big and vital into print, and from seeing one's own printed words reach the hearts and minds of readers.
>
> —Lucy McCormick Calkins

We have developed a sample time line to help you plan a successful school-level festival. Your own needs will undoubtedly result in some customizing, but this time line will give you a framework for organizing the many pieces of the puzzle. Young authors' festivals sometimes focus only on the writing of a group of children. At other times, they also involve a guest author, perhaps a children's book author, a newspaper reporter, or an author from a local high school or university. To keep the procedures clear, in this chapter we show what is needed for the basic school-level festival with student authors as the main attraction, and what is needed if a guest is part of the celebration. Tips for classroom-level conferences are included as boxes.

 **Six Months Before Festival**

For school-level festivals, you really do need to start planning six months in advance! If you don't have that much time, you may still decide to proceed, but you'll be wise to plan which details you can omit so that you do not become overwhelmed.

Classroom-Level Festivals

From one teacher: "My school always participates in a countywide young authors' festival. But my grade is never included. So I hold a young authors' tea of my own!" Whenever a teacher holds a classroom-level festival, the logistical management will be simpler than that of a school-level festival, but the teacher has much to do without the help of a committee. Allow at least several weeks to gather the writing samples, heighten excitement, and plan for parent participation.

◎ Basic Festival Procedures

You will begin planning for a school-level festival by obtaining approval and, hopefully, strong support from your principal. Then you are ready to convene a committee, establish a festival coordinator, and set up a schedule of meetings. We will use "you" from this point on in speaking to the festival committee as represented by its coordinator. You may want to schedule several monthly meetings before the festival, more frequent meetings as needed just before the event, and a wrap-up meeting once the festival is over. Your schedule of meetings will undoubtedly change as you go along, but meetings are much more likely to be well attended if there is a mutually agreed-upon schedule.

- ✓ Building principal on board.
- ✓ Festival administration plan established.
- ✓ Tentative meeting schedule set.

Classroom-Level Festivals

Action plans are also great for helping busy classroom teachers remember all they must do for their own young authors' celebrations!

The next order of business is to help the busy people you work with get organized. Thus, provide all committee members with a three-ring binder with pockets. Ask that all handouts be three-hole-punched, and plan to bring a three-hole punch to each meeting for those who forget. As soon as possible, provide committee members action plan sheets. Here is a sample portion of one:

Action Plan: Student Writing Committee

What needs to be done?	Steps?	Who will do it?	Cost?	Due date
Prepare and use writing rubrics.	• Prepare writing rubrics.	Writing committee		September 30
	• Provide workshop and distribute rubric to teachers.	Curriculum specialist	Refreshments: $XX	October 7
Improve student writing.	• Encourage authentic audiences (pen pals, cross-grade groupings, writing to school staff, etc.).	Principal, curriculum specialist		Ongoing
	• Encourage author studies to highlight authors' craft.	Media specialist		Ongoing
	• Involve students in daily writing through all stages of process writing.	Teachers, with help of curriculum specialist		Ongoing
Involve parents.	• Create classroom environments rich in language and literature.	Teachers, with help of curriculum specialist		Ongoing
	• Provide writers' workshop for parents.	Curriculum specialist, principal		November 1
	• Include student writing samples in school newsletters along with writing tips.	Curriculum specialist, teachers		Ongoing

✓ Organized binders with action plans ready for use.

During meetings you'll have a lot to do. Here are subjects you need to consider.

Determine the Logistics for Your Festival

- **Type of festival(s)** What type of festival will you have? One in every class? A school-wide event? What will you call it? An authors' tea? A young authors' festival? Will it have a student-author focus or be an event surrounding a presentation by an outside author? Or will you hold a series of festivals throughout the year to allow for participation from a broader range of students than may be possible with a single festival?

- **Number of young authors** How many students will be able to participate? You want to encourage all students to be authors, yet you may not be able to accommodate all students at one time. If you must limit numbers, how will you choose students while making sure that those who are often left out of the "literacy club" have a chance at participating? One classroom teacher limits the number of participants by having students choose whether to participate. Those who wait until too late are unable to complete their writing and be a part.

- **Date, time, and location** What would be a good date that doesn't interfere with other school events? Can the festival be held at a time convenient for parents? Where can it be held? You will want as comfortable and attractive an area as possible, perhaps the school media center. You may need a large area for a general gathering as well as flexible spacing to allow for authors to read to small groups. Darcy Cleek, a fifth-grade teacher, holds one authors' tea per quarter. She notes that "Those who share the first time will truly feel like authors and will be excited to make their next publication even better."

- **Costs** Figure out your festival costs and determine how the event can be funded. There need not be any real expense for a small-scale festival. But your plans can add up to significant costs, such as for food, printing, awards, and even perhaps an author visit. If costs do mount up, you'll need to ask for help from the principal, the PTO/PTA, and/or local businesses. If all else fails, try writing a grant. Some local grants are surprisingly easy to get.

- **Organizational structure** Will the festival be organized by one person, perhaps a reading, curriculum, or media specialist? Or will there be a leader working with a committee? It is sometimes difficult for all to feel ownership when an event is primarily on the shoulders of one person, but this organization may be necessary if committee meeting time is too great of a burden. When you consider ownership, remember to include special-area teachers. For example, a music, art, or physical education teacher might participate in the student author committee, helping students who want to write about subjects in these fields or, in the case of the art teacher, needing direction for book illustration. Consider also asking an art or music teacher for decorations or musical entertainment respectively. For classroom-level festivals, consider forming committees of students, for example, for program design, quality control (proofreading), and hospitality (invitations, escorts, refreshments, thank-yous).

Consider the following possible committees with their respective responsibilities. On page 74 in the Appendix is a sample checklist for the major planning steps to be followed regardless of whether the festival is managed by a committee or by one person. Also in the Appendix are sample forms for use by committee members.

Student Writing Committee

Before the Festival	During/After the Festival

Teacher involvement:

- Maximize quality of student writing by encouraging use of writers' workshop, word walls, and modeling of authors' craft; encourage authentic writing audiences.
- To encourage bilingualism and biliteracy, use teachers proficient in a second language to work, if possible, with young authors in languages besides English.

Parent involvement:

- Hold writing workshop in which parents themselves engage in process writing.
- Include samples of student writing progress and tips in school newsletter.

Rubrics:

- Prepare writing rubrics appropriate for each grade.
- Hold workshop to distribute rubrics and allow for practice in their use.

Outside Author Committee (Optional)

Before the Festival	During/After the Festival
• Bring author possibilities to committee. • Make arrangements with author. • Obtain and share author's books and biographical information. • Maximize student knowledge about author (e.g., through student book talks and bulletin boards).	• Make sure author has companion and • introducer on day of event. • Be sure author is paid. • Arrange for student-authored thank-you letters.

Public Relations Committee

Before the Festival	During/After the Festival
• Keep principal and all school staff informed.	• Oversee distribution of certificates and/or souvenirs.

- If festival is selective, give teachers writing rubrics and collect submitted writings.
- Provide advertising press release for school newsletter and community newspaper.
- Arrange for certificates and/or souvenirs of event for young authors.

- Provide follow-up write-up for school newsletter and community newspaper.

Historian Committee

Before the Festival

- Have previous records available for consultation.
- Keep new records in order.

During/After the Festival

- Develop film after event.
- File all records for use with next year's festival.

Hospitality Committee

Before the Festival

- Make and distribute signs and any decorations.
- Arrange for guest escorts.
- Prepare evaluation forms.

During/After the Festival

- Monitor guest escorts.
- Collect signs and decorations.
- Provide, collect, tally, and share results of evaluation forms.
- Send thank-yous for all committees.

Secretary/Treasurer Committee

Before the Festival

Secretary:

- Keep and distribute minutes.
- Proofread all printed materials.

Treasurer:

- Organize fund-raising and work with school financial officer. If fund-raising includes a book sale:
  → Review quantities ordered previous year and place orders.
  → Count books when they arrive.
  → Prepare recording form and gather change (lots of it!) in preparation for book sale.

During/After the Festival

Secretary:

- Proofread all printed materials.

Treasurer:

- Carry out sales procedures.
- Deliver moneys to appropriate officer.
- Return unused books.

Bookshare Groups Committee

Before the Festival
- Assign book-share leaders.
- Prepare written directions.

During/After the Festival
- Monitor book shares.

Once your major logistics are set, action plans can be completed. Don't set the due dates too late. There's always the photocopier that breaks down or the committee member who breaks down with it.

✓ Major festival logistics tentatively decided upon.

✓ Action plans completed.

Keep Up With the Details

Sometimes initial enthusiasm is high, but then the details get lost in the onslaught of everyday pressures. Be sure to remind committee members of each meeting. Keep written minutes at least for yourself, as they can help move meetings along. Use of a computer during meetings can eliminate the need for later typing and ensure that minutes are all stored safely in one place. Minutes can be especially helpful when a previously made decision is brought up. You can simply point to the decision in the minutes and politely proceed to the next item on the agenda or invite further discussion if the committee has new concerns. Be sure to check on the status of action plans at each meeting. And, of course, involve your administrators every step of the way!

✓ Structure established for keeping up with details.

Between meetings, one major task is coordination of printing needs. See if you can get any secretarial help for typing and printing. And be sure to have at least two pairs of eyes proofread every piece of printed material!

Here are some of your likely printing needs. See the Appendix for samples.

- **First printing needs:** committee tools such as address list and action plans. If participation is selective, early needs will also include teacher information sheets and scoring rubrics, and congratulatory letters for students.
- **Needs close to date of festival:** press release and festival schedule form.
- **Needs immediately before the festival:** directions sheets for adult/student helpers, programs, signs, student certificates, and perhaps book sale record form and student evaluation forms.
- **Needs immediately after the festival:** thank-you letters or certificates.

✓ Plan for printing needs established.

🔘 Procedures Necessary If an Outside Author Is Invited

If you plan to invite an outside author, the first question is how to find one. You may have some local celebrities who can establish an especially personal connection with your students and for whom you will, as a fringe benefit, not have to pay plane fare. Or you may need to look beyond your immediate area. Here are some tips:

- Publishing companies may provide an author, particularly if you work collaboratively with other schools or professional organizations such as local reading councils or TAWL (Teachers Approaching Whole Language) groups. It is more feasible for a publisher to sponsor a speaker if the speaker addresses more than one group.

- Investigate dates when an author will already be in town, perhaps speaking at a bookstore or at a school district event. Or, team up with other schools for a series of presentations. This way, your cost might be significantly reduced or even free.

- You can obtain a list of publishers who maintain an in-house person to coordinate author appearances by requesting the "Inviting Children's Book Authors and Illustrators to Your Community" brochure and sending $2 and a 6 x 9 self-addressed envelope with $.78 postage to Children's Book Council, 568 Broadway #404, New York NY 10012.

- Keep your antennae up! One of us was once a reading supervisor and would keep in mind schools that were on the prowl for authors to inform them if one was available.

Try to find out if anyone you know is aware of any authors who might be available to speak to children. Some authors are, of course, more effective than others. Once you have settled on one or more potential authors, investigate costs. Author fees vary widely. Investigate sources of funding. When all these problems are solved, secure in writing a commitment from your author with the terms of the visit.

✓ Author selected.

✓ Author visit arranged for.

Then you're only half done! We've seen authors speak at schools at which the children did not know their books. Instead, obtain books by the author for read-alouds and student reading so that students are prepared to ask questions. Obtain and share information about the author to help students feel a personal acquaintance with him/her. You'll want not just titles of books, but the juicy tidbits that will help students really know the author.

You can get such information from the author, his/her publisher, or the library. One reference source, *Something About the Author,* can be especially helpful. Also, consider ordering books by the author that might be available for sale during a scheduled book sale or a festival day book sale and autographing session. The following are comments from two fifth-grade students who had the opportunity to interact with a visiting author:

> It's fun to meet authors and see how they came up with ideas. One of the authors went to the Arctic for one of her books. She saw a sperm whale and told of her adventures.
>
> I like the way the author planned her stories and put her books together.

✓ Information about author obtained and shared with teachers.

Two to Six Months Before Festival

As time goes on, you'll nail down the details. For example, How many adults will be needed for supervising and videotaping/picture taking? You won't be able to expect an audience to keep attention for too long a period of time. So you might organize small groups with each student author reading to the members of that group. This would help you improve on procedures sometimes used when students just show their cover and read the title. You may, however, need to set a maximum length of time allowed for each child to read his/her writing.

A sample young author festival program from Kathy Eckhardt's multi-grade primary class is included in the Appendix.

✓ Festival schedule drafted.

As you move along, you'll want to share details. The cafeteria manager, the office staff, everyone should be informed. If the event is to be selective, provide teachers with judging criteria appropriate to the grade level so they can share these with students. You will probably want to use a general rubric that applies to all types of writing.

✓ All school personnel informed of festival.

✓ Judging criteria (if necessary) established and shared.

Remember to regularly check status of action plans.

✓ Action plans checked.

 ## Two to Five Weeks Before Festival

◉ Basic Festival Procedures

Things should get into serious gear four to five weeks before the festival. One major task is fine-tuning your schedule. Another, if the event is selective, is that of choosing young authors. Be sure to have more than one reader on each paper and to have your readers practice using your rubric to be sure they are following it. Otherwise, you might have biases—such as spelling being the bottom line—which color evaluations regardless of a more holistic rubric. If you have two readers who disagree, use a third reader to help make a decision. After selecting student authors, send them congratulatory letters.

✓ Schedule fine-tuned.

✓ Papers rated (if necessary).

Make final plans for day of the festival needs. Here are some considerations:

Practice! Practice! Practice!
Speaking in front of a group of peers or outside audience can be intimidating. Provide time for students to practice reading their writing into a tape recorder, to a buddy, to someone at home, to the class in authors' chair, or to you. Discuss how their favorite authors are invited to read their works, and share some of your own writing so that students have a clear understanding about why we celebrate writing in this fashion.

Audience
A writing celebration is enhanced with an outside audience. Within the school you can turn to custodial or cafeteria personnel, administrators, other

classes, faculty who are not assigned to classrooms, or parent volunteers. Outside possibilities include parents and grandparents, business partners, university professors and interns, district personnel, and local writers. Before inviting an outside audience, prepare a list of response techniques that promote positive and supportive feedback. Students can post these and explain them to the audience at the start of the celebration. The audience will then be sure to view the event as a celebration and not a critique. Fifth-grade teacher Darcy Cleek notes, "I distribute programs before the conference. Under the name of each presenter, I allow room for answers to possible questions for each author."

Ways to Make It Special

There are countless ways to make a school-level young authors' festival special. Here are a few:

- **Wrapping up the writing in ribbons and bows** The writing can be made beautiful in any number of ways. The author can use varied computer-generated font styles and illustrations. The writing can be printed in commercially available blank books. Wallpaper stores might donate samples of wallpaper that can be used for book covers. Students can include their own photographs. They can be taught bookmaking techniques as described in Chapter I or to go beyond these to pop-ups or other types of books. The creativity of you and the children can be explored in endless ways!

- **"I Am an Author" badges** Students can create badges that show pride in authorship. These can be collected in a jar and then distributed when authors share their writing. Some examples students have created: "#I AUTHOR," "I LOVE TO WRITE!" and "I WROTE A BOOK!"

- **Peer response cards** Teachers can disseminate student-illustrated cards that invite peers to respond to what they heard or liked about a peer's writing.

- **Rewards** Authors can be rewarded with certificates (perhaps computer-generated) that are printed with messages such as

OFFICIAL WRITER or PUBLISHED AUTHOR. Rewards can also be tools of the trade: pens, pencils, special stationery (perhaps computer-generated), or markers. Kindergarten teacher Sharon Reynolds advised that the festival *not* be a contest. Rather, prizes can be given to all participants.

- **Other ways of making the event special** Consider whether to have refreshments. You might obtain a videorecording or photo coverage of the event. The music teacher may be able to help with some entertainment and the art teacher with some decorations.

Two intermediate-level teachers provide suggestions for making classroom-level celebrations special:

"On the day of the tea, set up a table in your room to add an elegant flair: a tablecloth, punch bowl, ornate tray and centerpiece, perhaps flowers in a vase. This sets the mood of anticipation and celebration! Be sure not to forget to set out the goodies just before 'tea-time.' We just finished a unit on mysteries. During our authors tea, we added dry ice to the punch to create a mysterious ambiance."

—Darcy Cleek, Fifth-Grade Teacher

"This is a big deal! Do little things to make it special and unique from other 'parties' that the students have participated in: tablecloths, certificates, special visitors."

—Karen Kelley, Multigrade
Intermediate Teacher

Check on action plans. Continue committee communication.

✓ Action plans checked

You can start advertising the event to stimulate student writing and to give parents time to arrange to attend. Send invitations to school administrators and other VIPs. Make a hallway display related to the event. Arrange for media publicity—it's always easiest if you work with editors who write for a local supplement and if you inform the media that there will be unusual photo opportunities. It's often difficult to obtain newspaper coverage, but you might catch a slow news day.

✓ Advertising begun.

◉ Procedures Necessary If an Outside Author Is Invited

If an outside author has been secured, arrange for the author's introduction, perhaps by a student. Speak to the author to determine any audiovisual needs and the author's desired audience size. Ask the author if he/she would be amenable to any prefestival communication with the school via e-mail. If so, plan to take advantage of this communication. Perhaps students (and faculty and staff!) who are the first to read the author's work can earn the right to e-mail him/her.

✓ Author plans finalized.

You will be tempted to include as many children as possible in sessions with an author, but authors are sometimes more effective with small groups. Your conversation with the author will help you establish an appropriate audience size. If the audience size is limited, students might earn the right to participate by reading the author's work and writing a persuasive essay explaining why they should be chosen. You might also obtain permission for closed-circuit TV transmission to classrooms not in the immediate audience.

On daily announcements have students or others do book talks about the author's work. If appropriate, student or adult storytelling of the author's stories would be fun as well. Be sure that the author's name and book titles are spelled correctly in any published writing.

✓ Author's work known by students.

⚏ One to Two Weeks Before Festival

◉ Basic Festival Procedures

You're on the home stretch! One to two weeks before the festival, ensure that all participating adults are clear as to festival procedures. The committee should run through the day considering, as applicable: teachers and students ready? any changes in food counts? film purchased and in hands of the photographer? supervisory duties assigned? certificates or other young author remembrances ready for distribution? student evaluation forms in order? Check on action plans.

✓ Festival run-through held.

✓ Action plans checked.

In preparing for the sharing at a festival, fifth-grade teacher Darcy Cleek advises to be sure to limit presenting authors to four or five during a one-hour festival, or it will be overwhelming. You might extend participation to other students by having student/reporters gather biographical sketches through interviews of the authors and use these for introductions.

◉ Procedures Necessary If an Outside Author Is Invited

If there will be a book sale and autographing session, decide on a secure place where autographing can take place without books disappearing. Be sure to have ample change and appropriate record-keeping forms. Lines form quickly with autographing sessions, so spread out attendance at the book-selling tables as much as possible.

✓ Book sale and autographing procedures set up.

 Night Before Festival

The night before the festival, set up the physical location. Be sure you have necessary signs, tables, chairs, properly working equipment, and any decorations. Anything to be given to participants should be organized and ready for distribution.

✓ Physical location and materials ready.

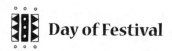 **Day of Festival**

◯ **Basic Festival Procedures**

Wear comfortable clothes, arrive early, manage by walking around, relax . . . and enjoy!

The following is a snapshot of one school's young authors' festival.

Pine Lake Elementary School in Miami, Florida holds primary and intermediate level young authors festivals each spring. In contrast to other schools, in which several children are selected to read their work to an audience, Pine Lake has chosen other ways of conducting the event. In one particular year, the primary K–2 festival was held on a Tuesday, with an evening repetition of the event for parents unable to attend during the day.

Picture yourself as a retired teacher, a grandfather of a seven-year-old. Your daughter has sent you copies of the two illustrated flyers she received, one for the day events and one for the evening repetition. The afternoon flyer begins, "You are cordially invited to attend a performance by young poets, authors and actors!! Join us in the cafeteria for a wonderful literary event!!! Activites will begin at 1 P.M." The flyer announces three event components:

- A Young Author's Fair with displayed writing from all grades in the school, preschool on up.
- "A Midsummer Night's Dream," performed by the gifted students.
- Oratorical Renditions, performed by the eight finalists from an annual districtwide oratorical contest.

You think back to the event the year before and of the school cafeteria displays—one decorated table for each grade level. The tables were laden with big books, accordion books, pop-up books, step books, class books, and shape books. You eagerly decide to return to the school this year.

Your daughter drives by to pick you up. As you drive in, she shows you the letter she had received asking for each child to complete, for homework, an original book or published piece of writing. She knew you'd be interested in the scoring details! The letter said that children would receive 50 points for the development of the book (prewriting, drafting, and revising) and 50 points for the final published book (story and illustrations), and that the overall categories of evaluation would be originality, audience appeal, illustrations, development of work, and mechanics. You and your daughter have a laugh thinking that neither of you had heard of children expected to write actual books when you were young children!

When you arrive at the school, you are given a program that you find impressive. Once in the cafeteria, you find that the event has grown so that now each teacher has a separate table. You head first to the table for your grandson's class, and you chuckle over his book. You see five-place winners for each class. The teacher in you makes you ask for more details about how the writing was scored, and the assistant principal gives you a scoring sheet. Five categories are listed, with each scored on a five-point scale. The categories are: originality (ideas are creative and original), audience appeal (writing holds reader's interest), development of work (beginning, middle, and end are used consistently), mechanics (punctuation, capitalization, and spelling), and illustrations (illustrations are consistent with content of story). You note that the winners will be invited to display their books at both regional and district-level fairs.

You then settle down to the performance and spend a most enjoyable afternoon. On your way out, you look forward to being invited to a similar treat for many years to come.

Should the festival be a classroom-level celebration, we can draw on the experience of Kathy Eckhardt, who teaches a primary-level multigrade class, to get a snapshot of a festival day. Kathy holds a celebration twice a year.

> One P.M. works well for my parents. Last time I had thirty parents for my class of fifteen. The kids wanted a *Where the Wild Things Are* set. We had both a general set and a bed. Some children used puppets. I always have a play and some singing. I was afraid that an hour would be too long, but the parents loved it. Sometimes the kids want to perform several pieces, but I have to make them choose. If they're short enough, they can do as many as four. The kids choose what they want to do. Some will read a favorite poem. The kids remembered "Pinocchio" from Shel Silverstein and took turns reading stanzas. One or more buddies may stand with the child and help him/her. One boy read his Texas haikus, done while he was in Texas on vacation. For the previous celebration we had been studying fables and fairy tales, so we had seen lots of those.

Kathy's students add comments of their own:

- We did poems; we did fables; we did songs and plays. Almost all of us did something from last year. We wrote a big "big book."
- I was master of ceremonies. I had to read papers between songs and plays. Introduce stuff and tell about stuff.
- We did a play and I was stage crew moving furniture on and off the stage for *Where the Wild Things Are*. (Two on stage crew.)
- Me and Chris did a poem, "Advice."
- It takes about maybe at least two months to get ready. (Kathy: It took a couple of weeks.)

Kathy explains some of the process: "We choose a topic. We brainstorm. We write about that topic. We do a rough draft. Then we peer edit, we conference, we do final draft, and then we publish it. We went really far back in selecting pieces we had written for the tea."

The following are two additional classroom-level comments related to the day of the event.

> Each author may choose three students who can share a
> positive comment about the piece. After the conference,
> I invite the audience to get autographs of each author
> and ask brief questions in short interviews.
>
> —Darcy Cleek, Fifth-Grade Teacher

> It's kind of amazing. People are so curious, and you're like
> a wizard, and they want you to tell all you know.
>
> —Fifth-Grade Young Authors'
> Participant

◉ Procedures Necessary If an Outside Author Is Invited

Turn in any moneys received from book sale to responsible officer.

✓ Festival held.

✓ Book sale moneys (if applicable) turned in.

One to Two Weeks After Festival

◉ Basic Festival Procedures

See the Appendix for tools you can use after the festival. Develop the film footage. Pay all bills. Evaluate the festival, using student evaluations and adult feedback. Record suggestions for next year's festival. Mount pictures and display, or show videotape. Plan to mail photos along with thank-you notes to sponsors. Celebrate!

Soon after the event, send certificates or thank-you notes to listeners and other participants. If at all possible, these should be written by the children. What better way to promote authentic reasons for writing? Help students write thank-yous that are well crafted. Pose questions such as the following:

- Share what you liked about having someone to read your writing to.
- What was your favorite part of the celebration?
- Tell about your feelings about writing: why you like to write, what you like to write about.
- Invite visitors to come back again.

✓ Thank-yous sent.

✓ Records in order.

⊙ Procedures Necessary If an Outside Author Is Invited

Return any unsold books to the publisher. Collect and mail student-authored letters to the invited author. Consider having teachers take the best letter from each class and revise that letter on an overhead projector to make it even better; these, then, could be the letters that are mailed.

✓ Any unsold books returned.

✓ Student thank-you letters mailed to author.

Large-Scale Young Authors' Festivals

The deepest secret in our heart of hearts is that we are writing because we love the world, and why not finally carry that secret out with our bodies into the living rooms and porches, backyards and grocery stores? Let the whole thing flower: the poem and the person writing the poem. And let us always be kind in this world.

—Natalie Goldberg

Young Authors' Celebrations: A Glance at a Day in the Life of a Young Authors' Chair

It's here, you think, but how did it come so fast? Another Young Authors' Celebration that culminates a year of planning. You wonder how time progressed so quickly and how you managed to find yourself up at 5 A.M., going over lists of volunteers. schedules, and last-minute tasks. You know that busloads of 1,100 children begin arriving in four and a half hours and that, once the activities commence, the day will proceed like a whirlwind until the final bus departs.

Your first stop that morning is the university's large group assembly area that will welcome the children, their parents, and teachers. By 7:30, some university student volunteers are beginning to arrive. Passing by their sleepy-eyed stares and the smell of their coffee, you head toward the signs that are labeled primary, intermediate, and middle school, for the careful arrangement of small groups of children. These signs are spread out in a semi-circle in order for the children to see what group they will be in. They will never know the hours spent arranging and rearranging groups to provide these young authors with the opportunity to meet and share their books with children from other schools. As soon as the signs are spread out, an orientation for volunteers takes place. University volunteers are assigned roles such as group facilitators or bus arrival/departure guides. You begin to place volunteers in pairs at each sign designating student groups. The volunteers will facilitate small groups throughout the entire day.

Without skipping a beat, you are now headed for the small meeting room where you disseminate name tags and begin another orientation meeting for countywide and university faculty volunteers. You think to yourself how grateful you feel to have this volunteer help. Moving eleven hundred children into small groups with a very tight schedule is no easy task. This group of volunteers is charged with facilitating university student volunteers and children with booksharing and with large group assemblies. They're fondly nicknamed "shepherds" and are assigned their flocks to watch over for the day. These volunteers assist with everything from helping lost kids and late arrivals find their groups to ensuring everyone gets a chance to read his/her book aloud during bookshare time. A few will be assigned duties of hosts and hostesses for guest speakers and authors. You thank each one over and over again and send them on their merry way as sounds of bus arrivals echo in the background. Next stop, bus arrival!

You quickly arrive at the bus arrival drop-off area to see that all the guides are in place and volunteers are safely escorting students, teachers, and parents to their groups. Campus police assist parents dropping off students and direct them where to park their vehicles. Looks good, you think to yourself. Now off to greet the author and prepare for the start of the event.

As you greet the author, Angela Shelf Medearis, you find in yourself a sense of wonderment similar to that of the children, knowing you are about to shake hands with someone who has written and published many books. Briefing the author on her schedule and answering any questions she has, you introduce her to the volunteer who will stay with her throughout the day. Somehow the whole event begins to take on a more realistic quality as you enter the assembly and prepare to speak to all who have attended. Facing 1,400 adults and children, you welcome them, introduce yourself, thank all volunteers for their help, and brief the audience on the day's events. You take a heavy sigh, step down from the podium, and release everyone to begin their Young Authors' Celebration.

Throughout the day you will wander from booksales tables to teachers' workshop sessions given by publishers and university faculty, to the keynote author's session, and to bookshares. One scene that stays with you as you move through the day is one bookshare, a little child proudly holding up a book entitled, "My Favorite Day," and reading it to the group. Little hands were then raised to tell the young author how much they liked the story and pictures, and the next child bravely stood until the whole process was repeated by everyone.

Another moment you hold dear to your heart is watching the keynote author sitting and signing autographs for these young writers. Bright-eyed lines of children eagerly waited for their moment, with books clutched in hand and minds full of questions. Patiently she answers questions, pauses for pictures, and smiles at the comments and questions that the children tell and ask. Looking at this scene, suddenly you remember why you were up at 5 A.M., why you spent the whole year preparing. This literacy event is embedded in your mind and your heart. You know you helped touch the lives of hundreds of children. You know they will remember this day just as you have.

Initial Considerations

Sometimes teachers are involved in large-scale young authors' festivals, perhaps for all the elementary and middle schools that feed into a particular high school. We saw a very successful example of such a festival in a community in which many migrant workers live, where fathers dressed up in white shirts to see their children's writing displayed on the walls of the local high school. Other large-scale young authors' festivals may be managed by a reading council, district office, and/or university. If you are the originator of a large-scale festival, you will do well by trying to obtain broad-based community support. If several organizations cosponsor, the manpower and womanpower can be rapidly multiplied. Of course, this means meetings and coordination. But it also means broad-based ownership which can help with effort renewal year after year after year.

> Gloria Plaza, reading supervisor, finds that the greatest value of the district Title I young authors' conference each year is not so much the writing product but the tremendous amount of learning on the writing process. An adult at each school, a volunteer teacher or media specialist, helps the students selected to participate with a number of edits. The children have an opportunity to organize their thinking. Children compete in primary (grades 2–3) and intermediate (grades 4–5) categories.

You may want a codirector if you represent one major organization behind the festival and there is a second responsible organization. Possible leaders include an officer from a local reading council, a language arts director from the school district, and a professor from a sponsoring university. Optimally, directors should commit at least two years to the project to help with continuity.

Beyond issues discussed previously for a school-level festival, here are additional considerations for a large-scale event.

◉ Scope of Festival

Some festivals might just host students participating in a summer camp for writers. The scope of the University of South Florida's Suncoast Young Authors' Celebration that we have directed is at the other end of the spectrum. It hosts as many as twelve hundred students from kindergarten to eighth grade from ninety schools. Because we want all children to see themselves as authors, our numbers reflect our choice of having a festival that is not selective. A fee is charged per student, and schools send as many students as they wish and can afford to send. Our students arrive in buses and by car. The listing of volunteers for our festival one year read: two hundred university students and two hundred other volunteers, including district personnel, university professors, school chaperones, and volunteers from other sources. Readers desiring copies of the forms we used for this festival, which can be adaptable to other large festivals, should contact us at University of South Florida, Department of Childhood/Language Arts/Reading, School of Education, 4202 East Fowler Avenue, Tampa, FL 33620.

We strongly recommend starting with something manageable and growing gradually over the years. You'll have to expect challenges, and the greater your experience, the better you'll be able to deal with them. We will immerse you in some of our quandaries to help you think through the scope of what you are able to undertake. First, we'll give you an overview of challenges we had with just one part of our festival planning—bag stuffing the final days before the event:

Friday evening a week before festival: Teams of university students help stuff books, folders, bookmarks, and other items into individual student bags. Be sure to keep primary-, intermediate-, and middle-school bags separate. Donated materials aren't all of the perfect amount so some bags get items that others don't. Oops, we're running out of bags. University bookstore can give us some. No sign of the adults who had been expected. Looks like we did order enough pizzas. Stuffing is taking place late because some enclosures had been late in arriving. Even so, some additional enclosures will be added at the very last moment. Sets of individual bags go into large trash bags coded for groups of students, as matched to a large chart. Try to use boxes to keep the bags in numerical order. Doesn't work—bags are too big. A few days later: Proofread the certificates printed with participants' names, and place them in the appropriate bags. Fix the errors. The bags start to tear. Rearrange the books in the bags to avoid this problem. Careful with that back problem! Energy running out with no time to eat.

The difficult task we had managing our Suncoast Young Authors' Celebration with twelve hundred students and four hundred adults left us asking how we might scale back. Volunteers who are willing to take on a piece of a more manageable endeavor are not always willing to tackle a responsibility for a group this size. Options include separating grade groups on different days, moving to selective attendance from each participating school, or hiring someone to help with the paperwork.

Putting together a successful festival can be quite exhilarating, maybe because you are skirting on the edge of danger! But a large-scale festival is a major responsibility. Enough said. Groups that work together on such events over periods of years can find the community that develops to be quite rewarding. Conclusion: Proceed at your own risk! (Now, who has ever been stopped by such a warning?)

◎ Subcommittees

Decide on the responsibilities you will take yourself, perhaps overall coordination and memos to schools, and decide on the committees you will need. Here are possible committees with their respective responsibilities.

Author Contact Committee

Before the Festival	During/After the Festival
• Bring author possibilities to committee. • Make arrangements with author. • As soon as it is available, include author information in memos to schools. • Arrange for companion and introducer for day of event.	• Monitor author visit. • Submit voucher for payment of author.

Student Bags/Folders Committee

Before the Festival	During/After the Festival
• Obtain donations. • Arrange "stuffing" party.	• Distribute.

Book Sales (or Souvenir Sales) Committee

Before the Festival	During/After the Festival
• Review quantities ordered previous year and place orders. • Plan sales procedures.	• Carry out sales procedures. • Deliver moneys to appropriate officer. • Return unused books.

Transportation Committee

Before the Festival

- Work with transportation department to arrange for bus arrival, parking, and pickup.
- Obtain and distribute parking permits and maps for buses and cars.

During/After the Festival

- Monitor.

Historian Committee

Before the Festival

- Have previous records available for consultation.
- Keep new records in order.

During/After the Festival

- Obtain photos/video coverage.
- Develop film.

Hospitality Committee

Before the Festival

- Obtain agreed-upon identification for helpers (visor/badge/button).

During/After the Festival

- Distribute identification for helpers day of event.
- Arrange for hosts at all workshops.
- Provide, collect, tally, and share results of evaluation forms.

Publicity Committee

Before the Festival

- Prepare and distribute advertising brochure and press release.

During/After the Festival

- Speak to any reporters.

Reception Committee

Before the Festival

- Arrange to have troubleshooters and volunteers to greet and shepherd students on day of festival.
- Make and distribute signs.

During/After the Festival

- On day of event, have early informational meeting for troubleshooters who will then circulate, checking on all aspects of festival.
- Collect signs at end of festival.

Secretary/Treasurer Committee

Before the Festival

Secretary:
- Keep and distribute minutes.
- Proofread all printed materials.

Treasurer:
- Open bank account with two acceptable signatures.
- Pay vouchers and keep all financial records.

During/After the Festival

Secretary:
- Proofread all printed materials.

Treasurer:
- Pay vouchers and keep all financial records.

Bookshare Groups Committee

Before the Festival

- Assign bookshare leaders.
- Provide bookshare leaders with written directions.

During/After the Festival

- Monitor.

Workshop Committee

Before the Festival

- Make arrangements with workshop leaders.

During/After the Festival

- Monitor.

Fund-Raising Committee

Before the Festival

- Work out and implement plan for systematic fund-raising.

During/After the Festival

- Work with book sales committee.
- Put together and present scrapbook/video to supporters.

Wrap-Up Committee

Before the Festival

- Decide on storage place for leftover materials.

During/After the Festival

- Send all thank-yous.
- Be sure closing reports from all committees are gathered and submitted to historian.
- Store leftover materials.

◎ Adults Needed for Day of Festival

Determine the number and type of persons needed for support on the day of the event.

- **Most responsible volunteers** Troubleshooters, author companion(s), bookshare leaders, and booksellers
- **Other volunteers** Parking assistants, crossing guards, food distributors, and chaperones
- **Multiple volunteer sources** University interns, faculty members, or booster club members; representatives from schools; reading council members; and PTO/PTA

◎ Secretarial Help and Printing Needs

Your needs will be magnified beyond those of a school-level festival in quantity of different forms as well as in number of copies. Consider producing an attractive tri-fold for fund-raising, volunteer solicitation, and general publicity. If you send letters to participating schools with school registration forms, you will need someone to respond to the volume of resulting phone calls. Another labor-intensive task can be making a roster of young author groups, especially if students from each school are divided into more than one group to allow for increased interaction. You will have some forms to print for committee use beyond those needed for a smaller festival: a list of sponsors for display, escort sign-out sheets, and a list of all helpers, responsibilities, and contact persons.

◎ Extent of Evaluations

Evaluation procedures can range from simple evaluation forms by adult and student participants to extensive data collection. Think ahead to yearly fund-raising efforts as you plan evaluation procedures. Envision a document in which you can cite quotes from happy consumers as well as increasing numbers of participants. Such a document can serve you well in future years when you solicit person-power and money.

◎ Fund-Raising

You will need a systematic method for funding your event. Use the combined brainpower of the whole committee to come up with possibilities. Fees might be charged for each child. These can be lessened if costs are offset with alternative fund sources.

Our college of education has an advancement committee for each department composed of community members and alumni whose focus is on fund-raising for departmental needs. In addition, we do a lot of "scrounging around." One year our sponsorship was as follows: plastic bags for student handouts from supermarket and university bookstore; lunches from fast-food restaurant; student folders, door hangers, and bookmarks from The Children's Board; cash donations ranging from $100 to $500, bumper stickers, books, and author sponsorship from book publishers; books purchased by school district; bookmarks from newspaper; and room for author from motel.

In general, we recommend three sources of funds:

- **Fund-raiser the day of the event** Try a book sale/autographing session or sale of souvenirs such as T-shirts. Try to obtain discounts of items to be purchased.

- **Donations from publishers, local businesses, or newspapers** Give photos to potential donors or show slides/video of previous year's event. Be specific about needs; this will reassure potential donors that moneys will be well spent. Also, let donors know how the public will be informed of their donation.

- **Cosponsorship** Costs of our festival have been offset through cosponsoring by the school district, the reading council, the university, and publishers.

◎ Incentives for Adult Participation

Consider incentives to encourage adult participation such as inservice points for teachers or extra credit for university students. Plan early for any such incentives, particularly if you plan extra credit for university students because university professors will need to structure courses accordingly.

Other Options

One often-used option is that of providing gift folders or bags for students, with writing implements, bookmarks, bumper stickers, and other donated items. Other festival enhancements you might consider are having a theme, using buttons/visors/name badges for adult helpers, and having musical entertainment or an art display from participating schools. Be sure to use action plans to help accomplish any such goals.

 **Cautionary Notes**

The following cautionary notes will help you avoid any potential pitfalls and have a successful event.

 Dates and Time Lines

It goes without saying that you must be very sure not to have a date which conflicts with other activities of any of the parties involved. A related issue is allowing for busy school schedules. If, for example, a memorandum is going to schools via school mail, time may be needed for the memorandum to be proofread, given or mailed to the person who will place it in school mail, processed through school mail, dealt with by the busy principal, duplicated and distributed to teachers, and read and acted on by the teachers. Allow at least three weeks for action that is simple, more if it is involved. If you need a response from teachers, factor in time for the information to be gathered, put in a mailbox, and processed through the mail. Failing to allow time is asking for trouble.

 Adequacy of Facilities

You have several issues to consider with facilities.

- **Rooms** How large? How many? Adequate acoustics?
- **Students sitting on grounds** Spraying for ants? Rainy day alternative?

- **Equipment** Tables and chairs? Microphone? Slide projector for invited author? Overhead projectors for workshops? Extra bulbs? Electrical outlets available?
- **Parking** Any fees? Enough spaces?

◉ Volunteer Reliability

Have extra volunteers on hand in case some do not show up. Also, consider pairing volunteers for selected tasks. For example, pair college education majors to facilitate book shares; this helps instill confidence and provides an extra person if needed, for example, to escort a student to the bathroom.

◉ Possible Lunch Snafus

We have yet to find a lunch solution that is adequate. The year when children brought their lunches we had difficulty getting lunches back to them at noon because we had students in cross-school groupings so that they could meet young authors from other sites. The year when we had runners pick up lunches donated by several local McDonald's, somehow in the scramble many were left without lunches—we still can't figure that one out. Bottom line: Think through lunch procedures c-a-r-e-f-u-l-l-y.

◉ Transportation Issues

School districts often use buses for several runs for elementary, middle school, and senior high school. As a result, young authors' festivals often see problems with late buses. Try to schedule major events after the first hour of the festival to allow time for late bus arrivals.

◉ Movement of Students

You may have during the day several times when students must be moved: to beginning site; between author presentations, workshops, bookshares, lunch, and bathrooms; and to home transportation. Sometimes you will have the option of moving adults or moving children. Although time is needed for children to move, you may want to select this option to help avoid fidgety children. If students are regrouped across school lines, you will, of course, need procedures for putting the pieces back together again. And dismissal procedures should be crystal clear to ensure that students are returned to the adults with whom they arrived.

 Time Lines for Large-Scale Festivals

Here we provide suggested checkpoints and committee responsibilities for all issues related to planning large-scale festivals. However, we give paragraph explanations only for details not discussed previously.

◉ Six to Twelve Months Before Festival

Large-scale festivals will undoubtedly focus on one or more guest authors/illustrators and on young author share sessions. You may or may not extend the event to include workshops for young authors and adults. Planning with and without such workshops differs especially at the early discussion stages. Here are some considerations.

Basic Large-Scale Festival

Begin by obtaining consent and, hopefully, active support from appropriate administrators and supervisors. You then are ready to lay the extensive groundwork necessary for forming a committee. Following are additional issues to address:

- **First committee meeting** For your first meeting, have enough in place so that committee members see that this will be an organized affair which will not waste their time. On the other hand, you will not want to assume ownership of any preliminary work and thus devalue the work and ideas of committee members. Have available for your binders for each committee member a list of committee addresses and fax, e-mail, and phone numbers. A detail to agree upon early is where the festival will be held, so have information on one or two available sites.

- **Site selection** Consider distance from schools when you select a site. For available sites, gather information on meeting room size, parking facilities, and any costs. If the festival is held at a school site, after-hour custodial pay may be required. If the site is a university, a certain number of parking permits may be granted. At university sites, it may be necessary to consider distance from parking to the meeting site; too great a distance and the possibility of inclement weather may make it necessary to plan for a shuttle service. Once the site is selected, make facility reservations, with written confirmation of room capacity and any other pertinent details such as availability of audiovisual aids and food regulations.

- **Student transportation** Plan for student transportation. Note logical spots for crossing guards.

- **Festival stationery** Make or order stationery with a Young Authors' Festival logo.

- **Action plans** When general logistics are established, work with each committee chair to complete action plans of committee responsibilities.

Festival with Guest Author and Workshops

A number of additional considerations are in order if you plan to hold workshops:

- **Workshop selection** Will workshops be separate for teachers, parents, and students? Parents might experience the writing process or learn how to make books. Students and teachers might be shown children's literature which exemplifies good design and illustration as well as writers' craft.

- **Workshop leaders** Who can serve as workshop leaders? Compile a possible list, for example, of speakers on career possibilities which involve writing, high school or university teachers of writing, consultants sponsored by publishing companies, PTO/PTA speakers, or guest author/illustrator delivering workshops in addition to his/her main presentation.

- **Workshop scheduling** How will workshops fit into the day? In planning logistics, consider number, length, titles, and scheduling of workshops, and travel time from one session to another.

Once decisions are made, secure workshop leaders and provide written confirmation along with map. Plan to have host in each workshop session for introduction of speaker, time control, handling of any evaluation forms, and general assistance.

Six to Twelve Month Checklist

Initial Considerations:

✓ Appropriate administrators on board.

✓ Scope of festival decided upon.

✓ Committee directions established.

✓ Date and location decided upon and confirmed.

Nailing Down the Details:

✓ Tentative meeting schedule set.

✓ Committee structure set up.

✓ Binders with vouchers, action plans, and address list distributed to committee members.

✓ Major festival logistics tentatively decided upon.

✓ Action plans completed.

✓ Plan for printing needs established.

✓ Author(s) and workshop leaders selected.

✓ Author visit(s) and workshop leaders contacted and arrangements made.

✓ Information about author(s) obtained.

Two to Six Months Before Festival

Two to six months before the festival is the time frame for laying much of the groundwork for a successful event.

- Send first mail-out to schools advertising festival, providing a phone number at which questions can be answered, requesting a school contact person and response as to level of participation.

- For small group shares, group student names. You might want to mix students across schools to enable them to meet, share with, and learn from those they might never otherwise encounter. Organizing cross-school bookshares, however, significantly increases the logistics, especially if the festival is quite large.

- If no sponsor is covering the expense, make the author's plane and hotel reservations. Do them yourself to ensure that you have the best rates.

- Start an ongoing check sheet of items to remember just before the festival.

Two to Six Month Checklist

✓ Festival schedule drafted.

✓ First mail-out sent to schools and responses received.

✓ Bookshare student groupings organized.

✓ Judging criteria (if necessary) established and shared.

✓ Action plans checked, and check sheet of last-minute items begun.

✓ Author plane/hotel reservations made.

Four to Six Weeks Before Festival

Four to six weeks before the festival is a good time for the following:

- Mail a second memorandum to schools, a festival update. If festival participation is selective, give schools the list of selected and nonselected students. If there are to be workshops, (1) continue communication with workshop leaders, being sure they submit biographical information for promotion and introductions, and (2) advertise the workshops in this second memorandum.

- Prepare handouts for adults and students, color-coded for ease of reference on the day of the event.

- Make final scheduling arrangements.

- Arrange for any food for students and adults.

- Plan to gather any available walkie-talkies.

- Be sure you will have enough signs for all strategic locations in parking lot and in building.

Four to Six Week Checklist

✓ Second mail-out sent to schools.

✓ Action plans checked.

✓ Advertising begun.

✓ Author plans finalized.

✓ Author's work known by students.

✓ Festival schedule fine-tuned.

✓ Adult and student handouts prepared.

✓ Food arrangements made.

One to Two Weeks Before Festival

You're on the home stretch! One to two weeks before the festival you'll want to include the following in your checklist of last-minute to-dos:

- Place chaperone handouts in a folder with a table of contents if necessary. Possible inclusions: map of festival site; festival schedule; general arrival, lunch, and dismissal directions; and book-share directions. In "running through" the day with the committee, consider:
  - Security guards' early opening of facility
  - Tables for registration, book sales, speakers
  - Book sale recording procedures set up
  - Locations of signs
  - Early reporting time for supporting adults
  - Availability of vans and carts for moving materials
  - Logistics of getting in and out of building and between sessions
  - Arrangements for carried belongings
  - Restroom locations
  - Lunch arrangements for adults and students
  - Assignment of any available walkie-talkies
  - Secure area, if possible, for storing items for sale and other valuables

- ° If there are to be workshops, alternative arrangements in case a workshop leader is unable to attend.
- Prepare any folders/bags with gifts for students.

One to Two Week Checklist

- ✓ Festival run-through held.
- ✓ Action plans checked.
- ✓ Sale and autographing procedures set up.
- ✓ Materials to give adults and students ready for distribution.

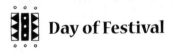 Night Before Festival

As with the school-level festival, be sure all equipment is in working order and all materials are in place.

- ✓ Physical location and materials ready.

Day of Festival

Meet early with adult volunteers to review responsibilities. Keep walkie-talkie handy at all times.

✓ Festival held.

✓ Book sale moneys (if applicable) turned in.

A fifth grade young authors' festival participant summed up the experience as follows:

> A neat experience and you get to learn a lot of stuff you didn't know. And you get to see what other kids and college students think and what they like.

One to Two Weeks After Festival

While the enthusiasm is fresh, write thank-yous. Along with thank-yous to sponsors send photos of the event, and request commitment to participate in next year's event. We are all more likely to agree to help when the event is far away in time. In a close-out party with the committee, discuss any required changes. If the festival had workshops, discuss with the committee which workshop leaders to invite back the next year. Other close-out tasks are completing a financial report and neatly storing all festival materials for historical reference.

Wrap-Up Checklist

✓ Thank-yous sent with requests for participation the following year.

✓ Records in order.

✓ Any unsold books returned.

✓ Student thank-you letters mailed to author.

✓ Committee wrap-up meeting and party held.

References

Professional References

Atwell, N. 1987. *In the Middle: Writing, Reading, and Learning with Adolescents.* Portsmouth, NH: Heinemann.

Calkins, L. M. 1994. *The Art of Teaching Writing: New Edition.* Portsmouth, NH: Heinemann.

Calkins, L. M. and S. Harwayne. 1987. *The Writing Workshop: A World of Difference (A Guide for Staff Development).* Portsmouth, NH: Heinemann.

Clay, M. 1975. *What Did I Write?: Beginning Writing Behavior.* Portsmouth, NH: Heinemann.

Radencich, M. C. and J. S. Schumm. 1997. *How to Help Your Child With Homework* (2d. ed.). Minneapolis, MN: Free Spirit.

Short, K. G., J. C. Harste, and C. L. Burke. 1996. *Creating Classrooms for Authors and Inquirers.* Portsmouth, NH: Heinemann.

Children's Books References

Aliki. 1986. *How a Book is Made.* New York: HarperCollins.

Babbitt, N. 1995. *Tuck Everlasting.* Boston: Houghton Mifflin.

Brown, M. 1996. *Arthur Meets the President*. Boston: Little Brown.

Cleary, B. 1996. *Dear Mr. Henshaw*. New York: Lectorum.

———. 1996. *Strider*. Boston: Houghton Mifflin.

Cushman, K. 1995. *Catherine Called Birdy*. New York: HarperCollins.

Ehrlich, A. 1996. *When I Was Your Age*. London, England: Candlewick Press.

Fitzhugh, L. 1996. *Harriet the Spy*. New York: HarperCollins.

Fritz, J. 1984. *Homesick: My Own Story*. New York: Bantam Doubleday Dell.

Gantos, J. 1988. *Rotten Ralph*. Boston: Houghton Mifflin.

James, S. 1996. *Dear Mr. Blueberry*. New York: Simon & Schuster.

Keats, E. J. 1984. *A Letter to Amy*. New York: HarperCollins.

Lester, H. 1997. *Author: A True Story*. Boston: Houghton Mifflin.

LoMonaco, P. 1996. *Night Letters*. New York: Dutton.

McCully, E. 1997. *Mirette on the Highwire*. Sutton, MA: Putnam.

Moss, M. 1995. *Amelia's Notebook*. Berkeley, CA: Tricycle Press.

Paulsen, G. 1997. *The Winter Room*. New York: Bantam Doubleday Dell.

Remy, C. 1964. *Fortunately*. New York: Parents Magazine Press.

Silverstein, S. 1996. *Where the Wild Things Are*. New York: HarperCollins.

Stevens, J. 1996. *From Pictures to Words: A Book About Making a Book*. New York: Holiday House.

Stubbs, J. 1996. *Dear Laura: Letter From Children to Laura Ingalls Wilder*. New York: HarperCollins.

Tate, E. 1995. *A Blessing in Disguise*. New York: Bantam Doubleday Dell.

Uchida, Y. 1995. *The Invisible Thread: An Autobiography*. New York: Morrow.

Van Allsburg, C. 1996. *The Mysteries of Harris Burdick*. Boston: Houghton Mifflin.

White, E. B. 1973. *The Trumpet of the Swan*. New York: HarperCollins.

Yep, L. 1996. *The Lost Garden*. New York: Morrow.

Yolen, J. 1987. *Owl Moon*. Sutton, MA: Putnam.

Articles on Young Authors' Festivals

Freeman, M. S. and W. C. Kasten. 1990. "A Secondary Model for a Young Authors' Conference." *Journal of Reading* 33; 356–358.

Gorsuch, S. and J. Fumas. 1989. "Strengthening the Reading-Writing Connection: A Plan for Implementing Young Authors' Conferences." *Ohio Reading Teacher* 24 (1); 47–51.

Harris-Sharples, S. H., D. G., Kearnes, and M. S. Miller. 1989. "A Young Authors' Program: One Model for Teacher and Student Empowerment." *The Reading Teacher* 42; 580–583.

Publishers of Student Writing

Send self-addressed stamped envelope with each submission. Note that submissions may not be returned.

Boys' Life. Boy Scouts of America, Box 152079, Irving, TX 75015-2079. Short stories or articles for boys (around 15,000 words). Ages 8–19.

Child's Life. 1100 Waterway Boulevard, Indianapolis, IN 46202. Short stories (1,000 words) and poetry. Ages 10–12.

Children's Album. EGW Publishing, Box 6080, Concord, CA 94524. Short stories (adventure, humorous, religious, romance, science fiction, fantasy, horror), 50–1,000 words. Fillers: short humor, crossword puzzles, sayings, cartoons. Ages 8–14.

Children's Digest. 1100 Waterway Boulevard, Indianapolis, IN 46202. Drawings and poems, jokes and riddles. Ages 9–12.

Clubhouse. Family Clubhouse Editor, 464 West Ferry, P.O. Box 15, Berrien Springs, MI 49103. Focus on the family. Poems (4–24 lines), cartoons, short stories (adventure, historical, humorous, but not science fiction, romance, or mystery), responses to editor's questions (e.g., "What's the funniest thing that ever happened to you?"), and some drawings. Submissions should depict positive family values such as bravery, kindness, and the like. Ages 9–15.

Cobblestone Magazine. 7 School Street, Peterborough, NH 03458. History magazine. Drawings, letters, and projects to "Ebenezer" with name, age, and address. Ebenezer also asks questions and publishes student answers. Ages 8–14.

Cricket. Cricket League, 315 Fifth Street, P.O. Box 300, Peru, IL 61354. Poetry, story-writing, and art contests. Submissions must be accompanied by a statement signed by a teacher or parent assuring originality and that no help was given. Ages 9–14.

Highlights for Children. P.O. Box 269, Columbus, OH 43216-0269. Poems, stories, black-and-white drawings to Our Own Pages with name, age, and address.

Jack and Jill. 1100 Waterway Boulevard, Indianapolis, IN 46202. Drawings and poems with name, age, school, and address. Ages 7–10.

Kids Magazine. P.O. Box 3041, Grand Central Station, New York, NY 10017. Short stories, poetry, nonfiction, black-and-white art, puzzles, games (400-word limit). Small honorary payments for published work. Ages 5–15.

National Geographic World. 17th and M Streets NW, Washington, DC 20036. Short writings about hobby or special collection for Focus on Collections column. Ages 8–13.

Ranger Rick. P.O. Box 774, Mount Morris, IL 61054-0774 (http://www.nwf.org/nwf). Fiction, nonfiction, puzzles on nature themes. Ages 7–12.

Reflections. Dean Harper, Editor, Box 368, Duncan Falls, OH 43734. Attractive poetry magazine published by Duncan Falls Junior High students. Accepts poems by students from nursery school to high school. Authors include name, age, school, address, and teacher's name in upper right-hand corner. Include statement signed by author and teacher or parent attesting to the originality of the poetry. Payment is a copy of Reflections. Grades 6–12.

Shoe Tree: The Literary Magazine by and for Children. 215 Valle el Sol Drive, Santa Fe, NM 87501. A quarterly published by the National Association for Young Writers, "Helping Children Write to the Top." All stories, poems, and artwork are done by children. Holds annual competition for young writers in fiction, poetry, and non-fiction. Ages 5–14.

Skipping Stones. P.O. Box 3939, Eugene, OR 97403–0939. A multiethnic magazine that encourages an understanding of different cultures and languages, with an emphasis on ecology and human relationships. Artwork, writings, riddles, book reviews, news items, and a pen pal section. Work by children around the world. English and Spanish/English editions.

Stone Soup. Children's Art Foundation, P.O. Box 83, Santa Cruz, CA 95063 (http://www.stonesoup.com). A literary magazine written by children. Published by the Children's Art Foundation, a nonprofit organization devoted to encouraging children's creativity. Stories of any length, poems, book reviews, and art (in any size and any color), and photographs. Ages 6–13.

Storyworks. Scholastic, 555 Broadway, New York, NY 10012–3999. A literature-based magazine for Grades 3–5. Includes book reviews by students.

Tyketoon Young Author Publishing. 7414 Douglas Lane, Fort Worth, TX 76180. Approximately one book per grade level 1–8 published yearly. Authors and illustrators receive case scholarships paid as a royalty on each book sold.

 # Writing Contests

We Are Writers Too! Prose and poetry accepted on the basis of creativity, research, and originality, up to 100 writings published each year. Contact: Creative with Words Publications, P.O. Box 223226, Carmel, CA 93922.

Young Playwrights Festival Winning play by author under the age of 18 produced in the Young Playwrights Festival in New York City; all plays submitted evaluated in writing. Contact: Young Playwrights Inc., 321 West 44th Street, Suite 906, New York, NY 10036.

The National Written and Illustrated by . . . Awards Contest for Students, Winning book authors invited to Kansas City, MO, where the staff assists in final book production; royalties paid. Contact: Landmark Editions Inc., P.O. Box 4469, Kansas City, MO 64217.

Letter About Literature Essay Contest Expense-paid trip to Washington, DC, and luncheon at Library of Congress for winning authors of letter by students in grades 6–10 about how a book made them feel. Contact: The Weekly Reader, 245 Long Hill Road, Middletown, CT 06457–9291.

National Writing and Art Contest on the Holocaust Winning authors of poems, newspaper articles, stories, plays, essays, or research papers reflecting their views and understanding related to the Holocaust, recognized at a ceremony in Washington, DC, at the United States Holocaust Memorial Museum. Judging based on originality, content, quality of expression, and historical accuracy. Contact: United States Holocaust Memorial Museum, 100 Raoul Wallenberg Place SW, Washington, DC 20021–2150.

Professional Organizations

American Library Association
50 E. Huron St.
Chicago, IL 60611
Sample publication: *Book Links*

International Reading Association
P.O. Box 8139
Newark, DE 19714
Sample publication: *The Reading Teacher*

National Council of Teachers of English
1111 West Kenyon Road
Urbana, IL 61801
Sample publications: *Language Arts,
Primary Voices*

Other Professional Resources

The Horn Book
11 Beacon Street
Boston, MA 02108

Instructor
Scholastic, Inc.
555 Broadway
New York, NY 10012-3999

The New Advocate
Christopher-Gordon
480 Washington Street
Norwood, MA 02062

Teaching PreK–8
P.O. Box 54808
Boulder, CO 80322-4808

# Textbook or School Publishers

American School Publishers
P.O. Box 408
Hightstown, NJ 08520

Free Spirit
400 First Avenue North, Suite 616
Minneapolis, MN 55401
e-mail: Help4kids@freespirit.com

Harcourt Brace
6277 Sea Harbor Drive
Orlando, FL 32887

Heinemann
361 Hanover Street
Portsmouth, NH 03801–3912

Houghton Mifflin
222 Berkeley St.
Boston, MA 02116

Richard C. Owen
135 Katonah Avenue
Katonah, NY 10536

Rigby
P.O. Box 797
Crystal Lake, IL 60039–0797

Scholastic
555 Broadway
New York, NY 10012

Silver Burdett Ginn
250 Hames Street
Morristown, NJ 07960

SRA School Group
250 Old Wilson Bridge Road, Suite 310
Worthington, OH 43085

The Wright Group
19201 120th Avenue NE
Bothell, WA 98011

Write Source
P.O. Box 460
Burlington, WI 53105

Appendix

Action Plan

Committee _____ Chair _____

What needs to be done?	Steps?	Who will do it?	Cost?	Due date

Six Months Before Festival

____ Building principal on board.

____ Festival administration plan established.

____ Tentative meeting schedule set.

____ Organized binders with action plans ready for use.

____ Major festival logistics tentatively decided upon.

____ Action plans completed.

____ Structure established for keeping up with details.

____ Plan for printing needs established.

◉ If Outside Author Is Invited

____ Author selected.

____ Author visit arranged for.

____ Information about author obtained and shared with teachers.

Two to Six Months Before Festival

____ Festival schedule drafted.

____ All school personnel informed of festival.

____ Judging criteria (if necessary) established and shared.

____ Action plans checked.

Four to Five Weeks Before Festival

____ Schedule fine-tuned.

____ Papers rated (if necessary).

____ Action plans checked.

____ Advertising begun.

⊙ If Outside Author Is Invited

___ Author plans finalized.

___ Author's work known by students.

One to Two Weeks Before Festival

___ Festival run-through held.

___ Action plans checked.

⊙ If Outside Author Is Invited

___ Book sale and autographing procedures set up.

Night Before Festival

___ Physical location and materials ready.

Day of Festival

___ Festival held.

___ Book sale monies (if applicable) turned in.

One to Two Weeks After Festival

___ Thank-yous sent.

___ Records in order.

⊙ If Outside Author Is Invited

___ Any unsold books returned.

___ Student thank-you letters mailed to author.

Rubrics are tools that enable educators to evaluate students' work on a holistic scale and to diagnose areas in need of further development. The following are four-point rubrics adapted from rubrics we constructed with Orange Ridge Bullock Elementary School in Bradenton, Florida, and from the rubrics for the Florida Writing Assessment and the New York State Writing Exam.

We share our procedures for using rubrics with Orange Ridge Bullock Elementary to help first-time users of rubrics plan uses appropriate to their settings. We developed Orange Ridge's rubrics with a committee of teachers. A set of papers was gathered from each grade level in order to find anchor papers, or papers that the committee felt minimally addressed the four areas of evaluation (focus, organization, support, and conventions) at each scoring point. Thus, we gathered four anchor papers for each grade level. All teachers were then given the rubric for their grade level to help them envision the scoring of writing pretests that were being given schoolwide.

Under our direction, the teachers then used the anchor papers and the rubric to score the pretests. Two raters scored each paper, with papers reflecting discrepant scores going to a third reviewer. The teachers found the tool to be helpful in evaluating the writing strengths and needs of their students.

Kindergarten

	4	3	2	1
Focus	Illustrations focus on the topic.	Illustrations generally focus on the topic.	Illustrations slightly relate to the topic.	Illustrations are unrelated to the topic.
Organization	Pictures clearly indicate sequence of beginning, middle, and end.	Two of three elements (beginning, middle, and end) are present and in order.	No pattern is evident.	No pattern is evident.
Support	There is some attempt to label at least two pictures.	There is some attempt at labeling at least one picture.	There is little or no attempt at labeling.	There is no attempt at labeling.
Conventions	The label contains representation of first consonant sound or a sound that relates to picture.	The label contains some sound/symbol relationships.	The label is a letter string.	No label is present.

Grade 1

	4	3	2	1
Focus	Writing focuses on the topic.	Writing generally focuses on the topic.	Writing slightly relates to the topic.	Writing is unrelated to the topic.
Organization	Beginning, middle, and, ending sentences are present and in order.	Two of three (beginning, middle, and ending) sentences are present and in order.	Writing may show no pattern. It may be only one sentence long.	No pattern is evident.
Support	One or more descriptors or supporting details are present.	One descriptor or supporting detail is present.	There are no details.	There are no details.
Conventions	Temporary spellings are understood. There is some use of conventional spelling.	Some temporary spellings are understood. There is some use of conventional spelling.	Temporary spellings are rudimentary.	There is no attempt to use even rudimentary spellings.

Grade 2

	4	3	2	1
Focus	Writing focuses on the topic.	Writing generally focuses on the topic.	Writing slightly relates to the topic.	Writing is unrelated to the topic.
Organization	The piece is coherent and contains several sentences including beginning, middle, and ending sentences.	The piece contains two of three elements (beginning, middle, and ending).	Writing may show no pattern.	No pattern is evident. The piece may be only one sentence long.
Support	At least two descriptors or supporting details are present.	One descriptor or supporting detail is present.	There are no details.	There are no details.
Conventions	Temporary spellings are understood. There is some use of conventional spelling.	Some temporary spellings are understood. There is some use of conventional spelling.	Temporary spellings are rudimentary.	There is no attempt to use even rudimentary spellings.

Grade 3 and Above

	4	3	2	1
Focus	Writing focuses on the topic.	Writing generally focuses on the topic.	Writing slightly relates to the topic or offers little relevant information.	Writing may only minimally address the topic.
Organization	There is a logical organizational pattern (including a beginning, middle, conclusion, and transitional devices). The paper demonstrates a sense of completeness.	There is an organizational pattern, although a few lapses may occur. The paper demonstrates a sense of completeness.	The writing that is relevant to the topic exhibits little evidence of an organizational pattern.	There is little or no evidence of an organizational pattern.
Support	There is ample development of the supporting ideas. The writing demonstrates a mature command of language including precision in word choice.	In some areas of the response, the supporting ideas may contain specifics and details, while in other areas, the supporting ideas may not be developed. Word choice is adequate, but may lack precision.	Development of the supporting ideas may be inadequate or illogical. Word choice may be limited.	Supporting ideas may be sparse, and they are usually provided through lists, clichés, and limited word choice.
Conventions	The writer uses various sentence structures. Writing shows proficiency in the conventions of standard English as expected for grade level. Commonly used words are usually spelled correctly. Few errors may be present but do not interfere with communication.	Most sentences may be simple constructions. Knowledge of the conventions of standard English as expected for grade level is generally demonstrated. Commonly used words are usually spelled correctly. Most errors do not interfere with communication.	The sentence structure may be limited to simple constructions. Frequent errors may occur in basic punctuation and capitalization, and commonly used words may frequently be misspelled.	The sentence structure is limited to simple constructions. Frequent errors in spelling, capitalization, punctuation, and sentence structure may impede communication.

The Suncoast Young Authors Celebration
Instructions for Booksharing

The duties of a facilitator for a booksharing session are very simple. The most important duty is to see that every child in your assigned group has a chance to share a portion of his/her book with the members of the group. Asking questions about the creation of the book, or about the child's interest in writing is optional. Enjoying the children and their books is unavoidable.

QUESTIONS FOR FACILITATOR OF SMALL GROUPS

1. Why did you write this particular book?
2. Why did you choose the topic?
3. How long did it take you to write it?
4. What was your favorite part of the book?
5. Which was the easiest part, writing or illustrating? Why?
6. What kinds of changes did you make from the rough draft?
7. How would you change it if you could?
8. Did you like doing the illustrations?
9. Would you like to use illustrations in your next book?
10. Would you like to do another book?
11. Do you have a title for your next book?
12. Would you like your school to have a school-wide Young Authors Celebration next year?

LOCATION **TIME** **GROUP**

Thank you for helping with our conference.

Kathy Oropallo
Co-coordinator

BOOKSALES RECORD SHEET

List of Titles	Cost	# Available	Tally	# of Books Remaining
TOTALS				

What did you like best about the young authors' festival?

What did you like least about the young authors' festival?

What suggestions do you have to improve the young authors' festival?

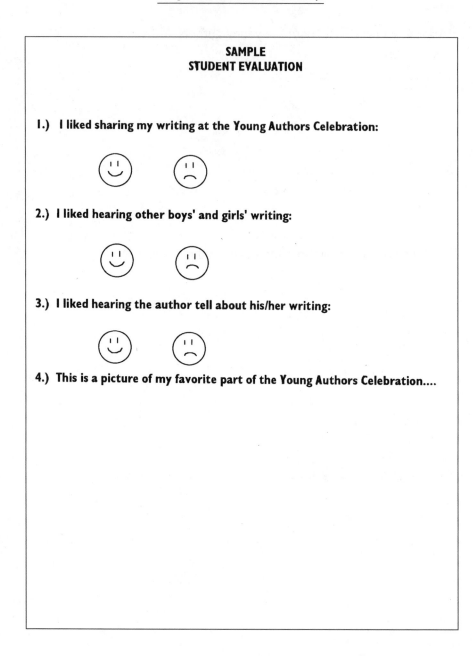

SAMPLE
STUDENT EVALUATION

1.) I liked sharing my writing at the Young Authors Celebration:

2.) I liked hearing other boys' and girls' writing:

3.) I liked hearing the author tell about his/her writing:

4.) This is a picture of my favorite part of the Young Authors Celebration....

**SAMPLE
STUDENT EVALUATION**

I.) This is what I learned from going to the Young Authors Celebration:

2.) What I liked best about the Young Authors Celebration was:

3.) I have these great new ideas for the next Young Authors Celebration:

My Ideas.......

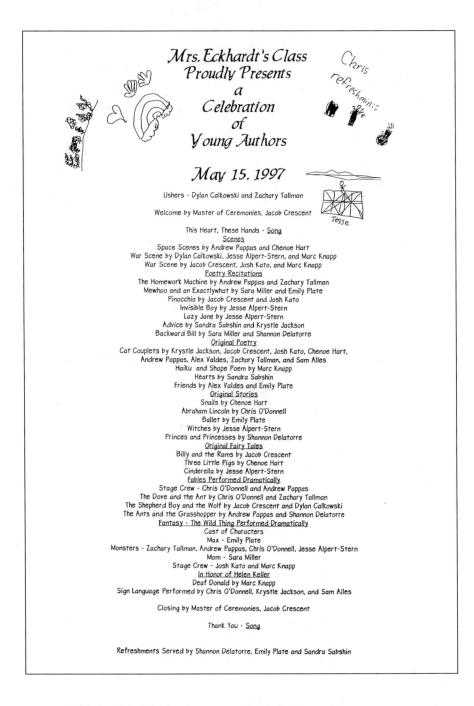

Mrs. Eckhardt's Class
Proudly Presents
a
Celebration
of
Young Authors

May 15, 1997

Ushers - Dylan Calkowski and Zachary Tallman

Welcome by Master of Ceremonies, Jacob Crescent

This Heart, These Hands - <u>Song</u>
<u>Scenes</u>
Space Scenes by Andrew Pappas and Chenoe Hart
War Scene by Dylan Calkowski, Jesse Alpert-Stern, and Marc Knapp
War Scene by Jacob Crescent, Josh Kato, and Marc Knapp
<u>Poetry Recitations</u>
The Homework Machine by Andrew Pappas and Zachary Tallman
Mewhoo and an Exactlywhat by Sara Miller and Emily Plate
Pinocchio by Jacob Crescent and Josh Kato
Invisible Boy by Jesse Alpert-Stern
Lazy Jane by Jesse Alpert-Stern
Advice by Sandra Sabshin and Krystle Jackson
Backward Bill by Sara Miller and Shannon Delatorre
<u>Original Poetry</u>
Cat Couplets by Krystle Jackson, Jacob Crescent, Josh Kato, Chenoe Hart,
Andrew Pappas, Alex Valdes, Zachary Tallman, and Sam Alles
Haiku and Shape Poem by Marc Knapp
Hearts by Sandra Sabshin
Friends by Alex Valdes and Emily Plate
<u>Original Stories</u>
Snails by Chenoe Hart
Abraham Lincoln by Chris O'Donnell
Ballet by Emily Plate
Witches by Jesse Alpert-Stern
Princes and Princesses by Shannon Delatorre
<u>Original Fairy Tales</u>
Billy and the Rams by Jacob Crescent
Three Little Pigs by Chenoe Hart
Cinderella by Jesse Alpert-Stern
<u>Fables Performed Dramatically</u>
Stage Crew - Chris O'Donnell and Andrew Pappas
The Dove and the Ant by Chris O'Donnell and Zachary Tallman
The Shepherd Boy and the Wolf by Jacob Crescent and Dylan Calkowski
The Ants and the Grasshopper by Andrew Pappas and Shannon Delatorre
<u>Fantasy - The Wild Thing Performed Dramatically</u>
Cast of Characters
Max - Emily Plate
Monsters - Zachary Tallman, Andrew Pappas, Chris O'Donnell, Jesse Alpert-Stern
Mom - Sara Miller
Stage Crew - Josh Kato and Marc Knapp
<u>In Honor of Helen Keller</u>
Deaf Donald by Marc Knapp
Sign Language Performed by Chris O'Donnell, Krystle Jackson, and Sam Alles

Closing by Master of Ceremonies, Jacob Crescent

Thank You - <u>Song</u>

Refreshments Served by Shannon Delatorre, Emily Plate and Sandra Sabshin

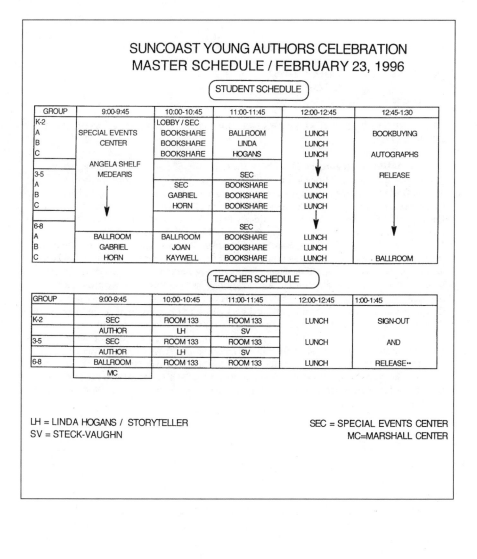

SUNCOAST YOUNG AUTHORS CELEBRATION
MASTER SCHEDULE / FEBRUARY 23, 1996

STUDENT SCHEDULE

GROUP	9:00-9:45	10:00-10:45	11:00-11:45	12:00-12:45	12:45-1:30
K-2		LOBBY / SEC			
A	SPECIAL EVENTS	BOOKSHARE	BALLROOM	LUNCH	BOOKBUYING
B	CENTER	BOOKSHARE	LINDA	LUNCH	
C		BOOKSHARE	HOGANS	LUNCH	AUTOGRAPHS
	ANGELA SHELF			↓	
3-5	MEDEARIS		SEC		RELEASE
A		SEC	BOOKSHARE	LUNCH	
B	↓	GABRIEL	BOOKSHARE	LUNCH	
C		HORN	BOOKSHARE	LUNCH	
6-8			SEC		↓
A	BALLROOM	BALLROOM	BOOKSHARE	LUNCH	
B	GABRIEL	JOAN	BOOKSHARE	LUNCH	
C	HORN	KAYWELL	BOOKSHARE	LUNCH	BALLROOM

TEACHER SCHEDULE

GROUP	9:00-9:45	10:00-10:45	11:00-11:45	12:00-12:45	1:00-1:45
K-2	SEC	ROOM 133	ROOM 133	LUNCH	SIGN-OUT
	AUTHOR	LH	SV		
3-5	SEC	ROOM 133	ROOM 133	LUNCH	AND
	AUTHOR	LH	SV		
6-8	BALLROOM	ROOM 133	ROOM 133	LUNCH	RELEASE**
	MC				

LH = LINDA HOGANS / STORYTELLER   SEC = SPECIAL EVENTS CENTER
SV = STECK-VAUGHN   MC=MARSHALL CENTER

SAMPLE PRESS RELEASE

Story Source: I.M. Anauthor: 123-4567
                Joe Smith: 123-8901
Media Contact: Pat O'Neill

THE SUNCOAST YOUNG AUTHORS CELEBRATION: A SALUTE TO YOUTHFUL IMAGINATION

     TAMPA, FL (February 23, 1996) - The University of South Florida and Hillsborough County Public Schools will bring March in like a lion when 1400 children from Kindergarten through Grade 8 converge on the University campus to attend the Suncoast Young Authors Celebration on March 3rd. This celebration of literacy, thanks to a partnership between the University of South Florida, Hillsborough County Public Schools, and Florida Educational Paperbacks, invites young authors to come together to share their books and drawings. Internationally known author of the book Stone Fox, John Reynolds Gardiner, will speak to these children sharing many personal insights into the art of writing. Also speaking on that day will be internationally known animator Trey Finney, who currently works at Disney MGM studios and has produced works in Disney films such as Aladdin, Beauty and the Beast, Lion King, and their new release this summer, Pocahontas. Teacher workshops will be provided by the Steck-Vaughn Company, who publishes children's work, and storyteller Linda Hogans, to encourage the ongoing development of children's literacy and to continue a county-wide salute to youthful imagination.

     This celebration was possible through the generous sponsorship of top contributors such as Florida Educational Paperbacks, whose cash and gifts totaled over $4000; the Banyan Foundation and Paragon Cable who each donated $1000; Houghton Mifflin who donated $500, as well as the Hunter's Green community association who contributed $350. Other sponsorship has been provided by Harcourt Brace, Josten's Learning, Scholastic, Steck-Vaughn, Troll, Walmart/SAMS, and The Wright Group.

Suncoast Young Authors' Celebration

Dear Principals, Teachers, and Media Specialists:

Enclosed are the final documents you will need to distribute to chaperones and students attending the Suncoast Young Authors' Celebration on March 3, 1995. We look forward to your participation. We believe this year's celebration will be unique. Suncoast Authors' Celebration will have over 95 schools participating with nearly 1,400 children from kindergarten through eighth grade.

You should find the following items in your envelope: a fee receipt, name tags with group assignments, information on the teacher/parent seminars available, program information, Young Authors' invitations, two parking permits, and a campus map. If your school sent in illustrations for the Hall of Fame, the certificates will be returned to your school with the illustrations. You will receive the young authors' and illustrators' certificates the day of the celebration.

What should you bring? Each student should bring the book, the name tag, a bag lunch and drink, and book money (optional). Florida Educational Paperbacks will have two book tables for students who wish to purchase books at a 25% discount. Drinks will be supplied for the students. Teachers need to pack lunches in a box with school name on the outside. We will store these boxes on the first floor of the College of Education. Lunches should not be left in buses or cars since parking is not close to the College of Education.

Can food be purchased at the celebration? Subway is located in the College of Arts and Sciences–Cooper Building. There will be other small food carts available. Use these facilities as a last resort because of long lines during lunch period.

Are there parent and teacher seminars? Yes! A Stock-Vaughn Company consultant will train chaperones in techniques of children's writing. Linda Hogan, a gifted storyteller, will share wonderful ideas about the gift of storytelling and ways to encourage young people in this activity. You will find a program schedule in the packet. Plan to visit both of the seminars at your scheduled time. Please remember we need you during the lunch period and booksharing.

As chaperones, what are our responsibilities? We will have 1,400 children divided into groups of 12–15. We need your assistance as we move these students from building to building. Please stay with your students and assist the USF teachers. This is especially important during the booksharing time. Every group will be divided into two teams of seven students. You will be asked to sit with one team and encourage each child to share a portion of his/her book. USF personnel will be available to assist you during this important time. We also need you to supervise your students during lunch.

When can we purchase books? Florida Educational Paperbacks will have book tables set up at convenient locations. You may purchase materials at a 25% discount any time during the celebration. We are asking that students use part of their lunchtime to purchase books. Florida Educational Paperbacks has provided a list of books that are useful in the classroom literature program. You will find this list in your teacher information packet that will be provided at the celebration.

How do we deliver students? Cars will unload on Elm Street in front of the College of Education. USF College of Education students and teachers will be holding group number signs. Students need to be assisted by their teachers to find the appropriate group. The name tags will have the group number on it. A school bus will enter the campus from the intersection directly in front of the Museum of Science and Industry. Head straight to the Sundome parking lot. A reserved area for parking will be available. Walk your children to the grassy area north of the Business Building. USF police officers and parking service personnel will be assisting the children as they cross the parking lot and street.

IT IS MOST IMPORTANT THAT YOUR GROUP ARRIVES ON TIME. THE FIRST SEMINAR BEGINS PROMPTLY AT 9:30 A.M. TO FACILITATE A SMOOTH REGISTRATION. THE CELEBRATION WILL OPEN AT 8:30 A.M. LATE ARRIVALS WILL NEED TO GO TO THE HELP DESK FOR ASSISTANCE.

When do we leave? The last seminar will end at 1:10 P.M. Cars should be lined up on Elm Street ready to receive the students. Bus students will line up and walk back to the Sundome parking lot. Police officers and parking service personnel will assist. It is most important that the groups be ready to leave quickly. Traffic officers will assist with traffic flow.

Where do I park? The closest parking lot for buses and cars will be the Sundome. This parking area has been assigned to the Young Authors' Celebration. Maps have been provided in your packets.

Can last minute substitutions be made? No. It is most difficult to have students attend who have not previously registered. Please make every effort to preregister every participant.

What will be the lunch procedure? With good weather, we are planning to eat lunch on the grounds. Primary students may eat directly in front of the College of Education on a large grassy area. Intermediate students may eat in front of the University Lecture Hall, a building directly to the east of the College of Education. Middle-school students may eat across Elm Street in the grassy area next to the College of Arts and Sciences–Cooper Building. Your school may choose the most convenient location for your lunch. McDonald's drinks will be available at a central location. Garbage cans will be located in all three areas.

What happens if it rains? A rainy day schedule will be activated. There will be some movement between buildings. An adequate number of rooms have been secured in such an event. Encourage your students to wear rain gear if the weather looks threatening.

Will authors be available for autographs? Because of the large groups, we are not able to provide an authors' signing table this year.

What will each young author or illustrator receive during the celebration? A literacy bag will be given to every student. The bag will contain notepads, pencil, *Stone Fox*, *The Lion King*, a celebration folder from Florida Educational Paperbacks, a Scholastic book, bookmarks, a hang tag, and other gifts from publishers. Each teacher will receive a celebration bag with materials on storytelling, literature in the classroom, and publishers' gifts.

Where is the Illustrator's Hall of Fame? The Hall of Fame is located on the First Floor of the College of Education. Enter the building and proceed through the double doors. Student art will be displayed on the walls. Please encourage your students to visit the Hall of Fame.

How do my students participate in the Hall of Fame? Illustrations from your artists may be sent to Mrs. Carol Finch, SAC Building, Hillsborough County Schools, before March 1. We will return the art through the school mails on March 8. Certificates will be included in that mailing. Be sure the artist's name and school are clearly printed on the front of the illustration. Private schools may send illustrations to Dr. Kathy Oropallo, EDU 208B, College of Education, 4202 E. Fowler Ave., Tampa, FL 33620–5650 before March 1.

What if I have a group book with one student representing a class? We will provide a certificate of achievement for the student representative who attends the celebration. You will also find in your packet a blank certificate. This can be Xeroxed and used for your classes. We suggest the certificates be awarded in an assembly.

Over 200 volunteers are needed to make this celebration the best ever. You are an important part of the volunteer force. Please help us move the children quickly between the sessions. Be sure not to miss the Steck-Vaughn Company presentation and Linda Hogan's storytelling program. They were designed especially for you. After those teacher-training sessions, you can catch up with your group and continue their program.

If you have questions, please call us at 974-1053 (Barry Morris) or 974-1011 (Kathy Oropallo). Thank you for your patience as we answer your calls. It is difficult to reach you during the school day. Consider giving us a home number and we will contact you during the evening.